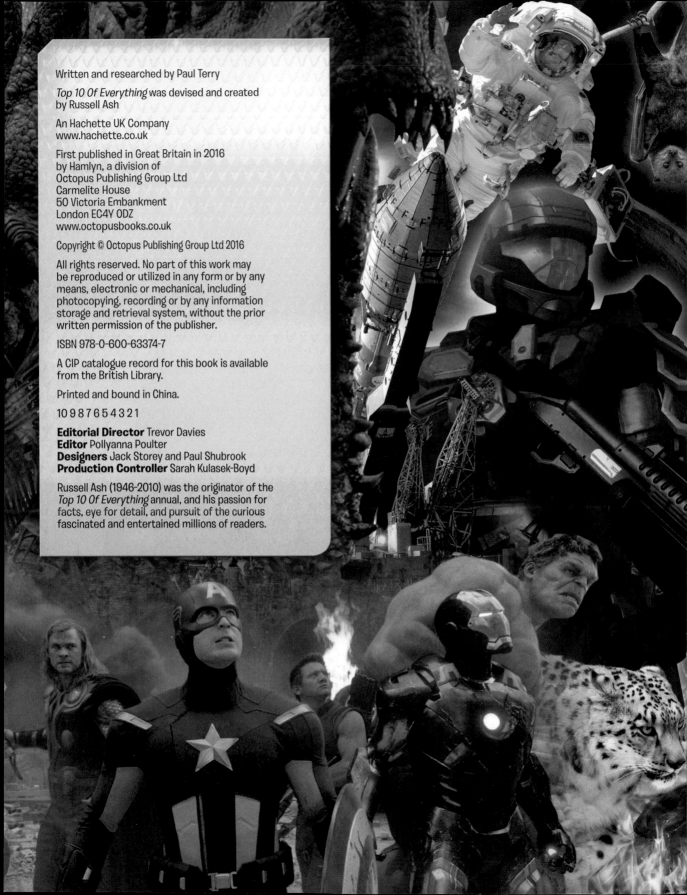

Written and researched by Paul Terry

Top 10 Of Everything was devised and created
by Russell Ash

An Hachette UK Company
www.hachette.co.uk

First published in Great Britain in 2016
by Hamlyn, a division of
Octopus Publishing Group Ltd
Carmelite House
50 Victoria Embankment
London EC4Y 0DZ
www.octopusbooks.co.uk

ISBN 978-0-600-63374-7

A CIP catalogue record for this book is available
from the British Library.

Printed and bound in China.

10 9 8 7 6 5 4 3 2 1

Editorial Director Trevor Davies
Editor Pollyanna Poulter
Designers Jack Storey and Paul Shubrook
Production Controller Sarah Kulasek-Boyd

Russell Ash (1946-2010) was the originator of the
Top 10 Of Everything annual, and his passion for
facts, eye for detail, and pursuit of the curious
fascinated and entertained millions of readers.

TOP 10 OF EVERYTHING 2017

BY PAUL TERRY

AUTHOR'S INTRO

Love Batman? But do you know what the biggest bats on Earth are? Adore BB-8? But can you guess which *Star Wars* movies are the biggest hits? That's where we come in. Other books are obsessed with weird "number ones", but we're all about the Top 10s. Of *everything*.

Inside these pages you're gonna find a bit of everything. With music streaming more popular than ever, we've got the stats that matter the most from the music world. Fan of outer space? We've got the lowdown on planet Mars and humanity's plans to colonize it. Olympic and Paralympic champions, massive wolves, the most popular art galleries, the largest lakes... *Top 10 of Everything 2017* has over 10,000 facts for you to pore over.

If, like me, you also love sci-fi, you'll find tons of genre TV and movie facts in this tome. Yes, for the first time, our Movie zone now covers TV from around the world, too. Maybe you'll find something in here that will inspire you to write a novel or a screenplay? And if it features giant bats, remember us when you're famous.

ABOUT THE AUTHOR

PAUL TERRY has written and edited official publications for Bad Robot's TV shows *Alias*, *Lost* and *Fringe*, as well as for LEGO, Disney, *Star Wars*, *The Simpsons* and *Futurama*. He co-authored (with frequent collaborator Tara Bennett) *The Blacklist: Elizabeth Keen's Dossier*; *Sleepy Hollow: Creating Heroes, Demons & Monsters*; *Lost Encyclopedia*; and *Fringe: September's Notebook*.

Paul is also the author of the Top 10 book series. His eighth, the *Top 10 of Everything 2017* combines his love of comic books, creatures and pop culture. Paul was also the designer and editor for Anneke van Giersbergen's book *The Road to Drive*.

When he's not writing books, Paul writes music. His film scores include *Emily* (starring Oscar-nominee Felicity Jones and Emmy-winner Christopher Eccleston) and the award-winning chiller *Care*. Under his solo moniker of Cellarscape, his records include *Exo Echo* and the award-winning album *The Act of Letting Go*.

CONTENTS

ANIMAL
KINGDOM

ZONE **1**

Standing on its hind legs, a Polar Bear's height can reach **11.1** FT

TOP 10

BIGGEST CARNIVORES

If an organism eats another organism, it's made the criteria for this top 10...

	TYPE	NAME	WEIGHT (KG)	(LB)
1	WHALE	BLUE WHALE	189,999.4	418,877
2	SHARK	WHALE SHARK	21,318	47,000
3	DOLPHIN	ORCA WHALE	9,979	22,000
4	SEAL	SOUTHERN ELEPHANT SEAL	4,989.5	11,000
5	CROCODILE	SALTWATER CROCODILE	2,000	4,409.2
6	WALRUS	PACIFIC WALRUS	1,883	4,151.3
7	BEAR	POLAR BEAR	1,002	2,209
8	STINGRAY	GIANT FRESHWATER STINGRAY	600	1,320
9	SQUID	COLOSSAL SQUID	495	1,091.3
10	BIG CAT	SIBERIAN TIGER	465	1,025.2

BLUE WHALE

1 As far as our current knowledge of life on Earth goes, this oceanic mammal is the heaviest organism ever to have lived. It grows to up to 110 ft (33.5 m) in length with 13 ft (4 m)-long flippers.

SALTWATER CROCODILE

5 This ambush predator strikes its prey seemingly from nowhere. Growing to 23.3 ft (7.1 m) in length, this Australian and Asian resident attacks the likes of water buffalo and wild boar.

ZERO CONTENDERS

This illustrates just how big the Blue Whale is...

BLUE WHALE 418,877 LB

WHALE SHARK 47,000 LB

ORCA WHALE 22,000 LB

SOUTHERN ELEPHANT SEAL 11,000 LB

SALTWATER CROCODILE 4,409.2 LB

TOP 10

HEAVIEST **HERBIVORES**

Animals that live off vegetation, instead of hunting for a meat/fish-only diet, can be found here...

	TYPE	NAME	WEIGHT (KG)	(LB)
1	ELEPHANT	AFRICAN BUSH ELEPHANT	12,000	26,455
2	HIPPOPOTAMUS	COMMON HIPPOPOTAMUS	4,500	9,920.8
3	RHINOCEROS	SOUTHERN WHITE RHINOCEROS	4,000	8,818.5
4	GIRAFFE	ROTHSCHILD GIRAFFE	1,930	4,254.9
5	BOVINE	CHIANINA	1,780	3,924.2
6	HORSE	SHIRE HORSE	1,500	3,306.9
7	DEER	CHUKOTKA MOOSE	725	1,598.4
8	TORTOISE	GALÁPAGOS TORTOISE	417	919.3
9	GORILLA	EASTERN LOWLAND GORILLA	270	595.2
10	KANGAROO	RED KANGAROO	91	200.6

A Chianina's height can reach **6.6** FT

SOUTHERN WHITE RHINOCEROS

3 This African giant grows to a height of over 6 ft (1.8 m). Its name comes from a general description of its light grey skin colour (which can also be a muddy yellow hue).

LARGEST REPTILE FAMILIES

Taking into account all of the different families of reptiles, these ones are the biggest you'll find in each...

	REPTILE FAMILY	NAME	WEIGHT (KG)	(LB)
1	CROCODYLIDAE	SALTWATER CROCODILE	2,000	4,409.2
2	ALLIGATORIDAE	BLACK CAIMAN	1,310	2,900
3	GAVIALIDAE	GHARIAL	977	2,150
4	DERMOCHELYIDAE	LEATHERBACK SEA TURTLE	961.1	2,120
5	TESTUDINIDAE	GALÁPAGOS TORTOISE	417	919.3
6	BOIDAE	GREEN ANACONDA	249.5	550
7	VARANIDAE	KOMODO DRAGON	166	366
8	PYTHONIDAE	RETICULATED PYTHON	158.8	350.1
9	VIPERIDAE	GABOON VIPER	20	44.1
10	ELAPIDAE	KING COBRA	12.7	28

LEATHERBACK SEA TURTLE

4 Their diet is almost exclusively jellyfish. Although they lay their eggs (often over 100) on beaches, they spend the majority of their lives in the open ocean.

GABOON VIPER

9 Measuring up to 6.8 ft (2.1 m) in length, this is the heaviest viper. Its two front fangs can grow up to 1.9 in (5 cm) long.

Gharial have **110** teeth

BIGGEST PREHISTORIC BIPEDAL CARNIVORES

Of the fossils we've uncovered so far, these ancient meat-eating beasts are the largest...

	DINOSAUR	LENGTH (M)	(FT)
1	SPINOSAURUS	18	59
▶ 2	CARCHARODONTOSAURUS	13.2	43.3
=	GIGANOTOSAURUS	13.2	43.3
4	CHILANTAISAURUS	13	42.7
5	TYRANNOSAURUS REX	12.3	40.4
6	TYRANNOTITAN	12.2	40
▶ 7	TORVOSAURUS	12	39.4
=	ALLOSAURUS	12	39.4
9	ACROCANTHOSAURUS	11.5	37.7
10	DELTADROMEUS	11	36.1

TORVOSAURUS

7 This dinosaur was officially named in 1979. Similar in appearance to *Tyrannosaurus rex*, *Torvosaurus* also had two very short arms.

The largest T-rex tooth discovered to date is

12 IN

long

CARCHARODONTOSAURUS

2 Scientists estimate this meat-eating dinosaur weighed up to 33,290 lb (15,100 kg). Its teeth were serrated like steak knives, with the longest being 8 in (20.3 cm) long.

GIANT WATER BUG

7 A fearless predator, the Giant Water Bug attacks prey much bigger than itself, including small snakes, amphibians, and even young turtles.

TOP 5 COMPARED

Side-by-side, the 5 largest would look like this...

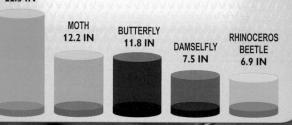

STICK INSECT 22.3 IN

MOTH 12.2 IN

BUTTERFLY 11.8 IN

DAMSELFLY 7.5 IN

RHINOCEROS BEETLE 6.9 IN

TOP 10

BIGGEST INSECTS

Comparing the different kinds of critters from the insect kingdom, these are the largest...

	TYPE	INSECT	SIZE (LENGTH) (CM)	(IN)
1	STICK INSECT	CHAN'S MEGASTICK	56.7	22.3
2	MOTH	WHITE WITCH MOTH	31	12.2 *
3	BUTTERFLY	QUEEN ALEXANDRA'S BIRDWING	30	11.8 *
4	DAMSELFLY	MEGALOPREPUS CAERULATUS	19	7.5 *
5	RHINOCEROS BEETLE	HERCULES BEETLE	17.5	6.9
6	LONGHORN BEETLE	TITAN BEETLE	16.7	6.6
7	WATER BUG	GIANT WATER BUG	12	4.75
8	FLY	MYDAS FLY	10	3.9 *
9	MANTID	GIANT AFRICAN MANTIS	8	3.1
10	WASP	TARANTULA HAWK SPIDER WASP	5	2

Wingspan, the rest are lengths.

MYDAS FLY

8 Like something out of a science fiction movie, the Mydas Fly is a true giant. Resembling a mutant hornet much more than a housefly, there are over 400 species found in hot climates all over the world.

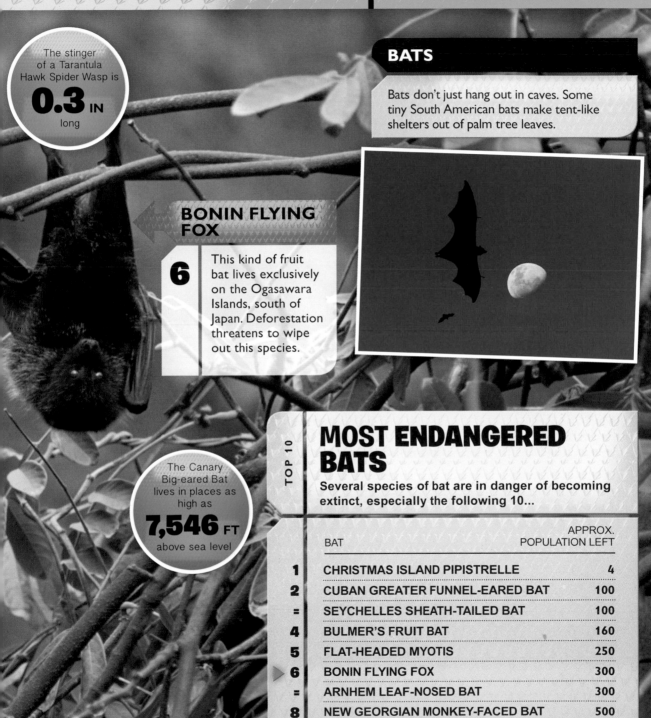

The stinger of a Tarantula Hawk Spider Wasp is

0.3 IN long

BATS

Bats don't just hang out in caves. Some tiny South American bats make tent-like shelters out of palm tree leaves.

BONIN FLYING FOX

6 This kind of fruit bat lives exclusively on the Ogasawara Islands, south of Japan. Deforestation threatens to wipe out this species.

The Canary Big-eared Bat lives in places as high as

7,546 FT above sea level

TOP 10

MOST ENDANGERED BATS

Several species of bat are in danger of becoming extinct, especially the following 10...

	BAT	APPROX. POPULATION LEFT
1	CHRISTMAS ISLAND PIPISTRELLE	4
2	CUBAN GREATER FUNNEL-EARED BAT	100
=	SEYCHELLES SHEATH-TAILED BAT	100
4	BULMER'S FRUIT BAT	160
5	FLAT-HEADED MYOTIS	250
6	BONIN FLYING FOX	300
=	ARNHEM LEAF-NOSED BAT	300
8	NEW GEORGIAN MONKEY-FACED BAT	500
9	THAILAND ROUNDLEAF BAT	1200
10	CANARY BIG-EARED BAT	1250

SMALLEST PREHISTORIC FLYERS

Although the prehistoric skies were home to some terrifying giants, other flying creatures were a lot smaller...

	PTEROSAUR	WINGSPAN (CM)	(IN)
1	IBEROMESORNIS ROMERALI	20	7.9
2	NEMICOLOPTERUS CRYPTICUS	25	9.8
3	PALAEOCHIROPTERYX TUPAIODON	30	11.8
4	ANUROGNATHUS AMMONI	35	13.8
5	ICARONYCTERIS INDEX	37	14.6
6	PREONDACTYLUS BUFFARINII	45	17.7
7	PETEINOSAURUS ZAMBELLII	60	23.6
8	CONFUCIUSORNIS SP.	70	27.6
9	JEHOLOPTERUS NINCHENGENSIS	90	35.4
10	ARCHAEOPTERYX SP.	100	39.4

ANUROGNATHUS AMMONI

4 Fans of the British sci-fi TV series *Primeval* (2007–11) will have seen this tiny flying pterosaur make more than one appearance during its five seasons.

Some experts believe *Iberomesornis romerali* lived

125 MILLION years ago

ARCHAEOPTERYX SP.

10 This pterosaur, one of the most well-known prehistoric flyers, weighed 2.2 lb (0.9 kg). Resembling a bird-like dinosaur, its name translates from Greek to mean "ancient feather".

GYRFALCON

3 These falcons prefer to nest on a cliff ledge, rather than build their nests from scratch. They are also known to reuse nests left abandoned by other birds.

FASTEST FIVE

Here is how the top 5 compare visually...

PEREGRINE FALCON 241.7 MPH

GOLDEN EAGLE 198.8 MPH

GYRFALCON 129.9 MPH

SWIFT 106.3 MPH

WHITE-THROATED NEEDLETAIL 105 MPH

Grey-headed Albatross's wingspan: **7.2** FT

FASTEST IN THE AIR

TOP 10

New data is in, which means we have some new speed-kings when it comes to the fastest birds in the world...

	BIRD	MAXIMUM KNOWN SPEED (KPH)	(MPH)
1	PEREGRINE FALCON	389	241.7
2	GOLDEN EAGLE	320	198.8
3	GYRFALCON	209	129.9
4	SWIFT	171	106.3
5	WHITE-THROATED NEEDLETAIL	169	105
6	EURASIAN HOBBY	161	100
7	FRIGATEBIRD	153	95.1
8	SPUR-WINGED GOOSE	142	88.2
9	RED-BREASTED MERGANSER	130	80.8
10	GREY-HEADED ALBATROSS	127	78.9

GOLDEN EAGLE

2 This bird of prey is the most popular national animal. It has been adopted as such by Albania, Austria, Germany, Kazakhstan, and Mexico.

TOP 10

BIGGEST BATS

There are many different species of these flying mammals, but these are the largest...

	BAT	SIZE (WIDTH)	
		(M)	(FT)
1	LARGE FLYING FOX	2.1	7
2	BLACK FLYING FOX	1.8	6
3	GIANT GOLDEN-CROWNED FLYING FOX	1.7	5.6
4	PEMBA FLYING FOX	1.6	5.2
5	GREY-HEADED FLYING FOX	1.53	5
6	INDIAN FLYING FOX	1.5	4.9
=	GREAT FLYING FOX	1.5	4.9
8	LIVINGSTONE'S FRUIT BAT	1.4	4.6
9	MADAGASCAN FLYING FOX	1.25	4.1
10	LITTLE RED FLYING FOX	1.2	3.9

GREY-HEADED FLYING FOX

5 This Australian bat is the largest found in the country. Weighing up to 2 lb (0.9 kg), they can live to around 15 years in the wild.

LARGE FLYING FOX

1 As this species feeds on nectars and fruits, it does not possess the power of echolocation, which many other bats are famous for using to hunt.

The Little Red Flying Fox weighs

18 oz

27

King Penguin's height:
3.3 FT

OSTRICH

1 This is the fastest flightless bird on the planet, achieving speeds of up to 60 mph (96.6 kph). They also lay the largest eggs of any bird, reaching over 3 lb (1.4 kg).

TOP 10

HEAVIEST BIRDS

Be they swimmers, runners, or flyers, these are the 10 birds that tip the scales the most...

	BIRD	WEIGHT (KG)	(LB)
1	OSTRICH	156.8	346
2	DOUBLE-WATTLED CASSOWARY	85	190
3	EMU	60	130
4	GOLD-NECK CASSOWARY	58	128
5	EMPEROR PENGUIN	45.4	100
6	GREATER RHEA	40	88
7	DARWIN'S RHEA	28.6	63
8	LITTLE CASSOWARY	26	57
9	KING PENGUIN	16	35
10	DALMATIAN PELICAN	15	33

DALMATIAN PELICAN

10 The largest of all pelicans, this bird has a wingspan of 11.3 ft (3.4 m). It favours a diet of fish, and its large pouch underneath its bill can be used to store prey it chooses to consume later.

Experts estimate there are over **10,000** bird species

CRIMSON CHAT

8 The Crimson Chat's egg incubation time is 14 days. This Australian species weighs 0.4 oz (10 g). Males have brighter red colouring to attract females.

STRIATED PARDOLATE

3 This species is found in almost every territory of Australia, except some of the desert regions in the western part of the country. They tend to feed on insects in eucalyptus trees.

TOP 10

SMALLEST BIRDS

Which is the smallest species of bird where you live? Find out and compare it to these, the 10 tiniest birds on Earth…

	BIRD	SIZE (LENGTH) (CM)	(IN)
1	BEE HUMMINGBIRD	5	1.97
2	BANANAQUIT	7.5	2.96
3	WEEBILL	8	3.15
=	STRIATED PARDOLATE	8	3.15
5	GOLDCREST	8.5	3.35
6	BROWN GERYGONE	9	3.54
=	LESSER GOLDFINCH	9	3.54
8	CRIMSON CHAT	10	3.94
=	GOLDEN-HEADED CISTICOLA	10	3.94
10	TROPICAL PARULA	11	4.33

TOP 10

BIGGEST BUTTERFLIES

These delicate winged insects are so large, when they are seen in flight, they are often mistaken for birds...

	BUTTERFLY	SIZE (WIDTH) (CM)	(IN)
1	QUEEN ALEXANDRA'S BIRDWING	30	11.8
2	GOLIATH BIRDWING	28	11
3	GIANT AFRICAN SWALLOWTAIL	25	9.8
4	RIPPON'S BIRDWING	20	7.9
=	WALLACE'S GOLDEN BIRDWING	20	7.9
6	PALAWAN BIRDWING	19	7.5
=	PRIAM'S BIRDWING	19	7.5
8	MAGELLAN BIRDWING	18	7.1
9	RAJAH BROOKE'S BIRDWING	17	6.7
10	CHIMAERA BIRDWING	16	6.3

GOLIATH BIRDWING

2 Males are smaller but also brighter in colour than females. They have green and yellow patterning, whereas the females are brown and yellow.

QUEEN ALEXANDRA'S BIRDWING

1 The largest butterfly in the world is an endangered species. It is illegal to capture and sell this butterfly. The male's wingspan can be up to 3.5 in (9 cm) smaller than the female's.

BUTTERFLIES VS MOTHS

Here is how the top 5 from each chart measure up...

QUEEN ALEXANDRA'S BIRDWING 11.8 IN

WHITE WITCH MOTH 12.2 IN

GOLIATH BIRDWING 11 IN

ATLAS MOTH 10.3 IN

GIANT AFRICAN SWALLOWTAIL 9.8 IN

MADAGASCAR 8.9

DEATH'S-HEAD HAWKMOTH

Just missing out on a place in this top 10 is the iconic Death's-head Hawkmoth. Its wingspan measures 4.7 in (12 cm). It was a key part of the case in the 1991 thriller .

WHITE WITCH MOTH

1 Moth fans may also know this huge species under one of its other names, such as the Great Owlet Moth, the Ghost Moth, or the Great Grey Witch Moth.

Atlas Moth caterpillar's length:
4.5 IN

BUTTERFLY

MOTH

IN BIRDWING

CECROPIA MOTH
7 IN

WALLACE'S GOLDEN BIRDWING
7.9 IN

IMPERIAL MOTH
6.9 IN

TOP 10 BIGGEST MOTHS

With over 160,000 different kinds of moth, these are the 10 that come out on top when comparing wingspans...

	MOTH	SIZE (WIDTH) (CM)	(IN)
1	WHITE WITCH MOTH	31	12.2
2	ATLAS MOTH	26.2	10.3
3	MADAGASCAR MOON MOTH	22.6	8.9
4	CECROPIA MOTH	17.8	7
5	IMPERIAL MOTH	17.4	6.9
6	BLACK WITCH MOTH	17	6.7
7	EMPEROR GUM MOTH	15	5.9
=	POLYPHEMUS MOTH	15	5.9
9	OWL MOTH	14	5.5
10	LUNA MOTH	12.7	5

LARGEST PREHISTORIC FISH

A school bus is around 45 ft (13.7 m) long, and many of these entries are at least half that length...

	NAME	LENGTH (M)	(FT)
1	MEGALODON	16	52.5
2	DUNKLEOSTEUS	10	32.8
=	LEEDSICHTHYS	10	32.8
4	ONCHOPRISTIS	8	26.2
5	RHIZODUS	7	23
6	CRETOXYRHINA	6.1	20
7	ISURUS	6	19.7
=	XIPHACTINUS	6	19.7
9	MAWSONIA	4	13.1
=	ONYCHODUS	4	13.1

ONCHOPRISTIS

4 This prehistoric fish is related to the modern sawfish, and little has changed in its biology over millions of years. Its barbed snout grew to a length of nearly 9 ft (2.7 m).

DUNKLEOSTEUS

2 Scientists estimate that this huge bony-jawed fish weighed up to 8,000 lb (3,628.7 kg). Fossils unearthed to date suggest there were 10 different kinds of *Dunkleosteus*.

An ancient ancestor of the modern Mako Shark, Isurus's teeth were **3.5** IN long

BIGGEST PREHISTORIC OCEAN BEASTS

Combining reptiles, mammals, and fish, these were the largest creatures in prehistoric oceans...

	NAME	TYPE	LENGTH (M)	(FT)
1	SHONISAURUS	REPTILE	21	66
2	BASILOSAURUS	MAMMAL	20	65.6
3	LIVYATAN	MAMMAL	17.5	57.4
4	MEGALODON	FISH	16	52.5
5	MOSASAURUS	REPTILE	15.2	49.9
=	HAINOSAURUS	REPTILE	15.2	49.9
7	ELASMOSAURUS	REPTILE	14	46
8	PLIOSAURUS	REPTILE	12.8	42
9	DUNKLEOSTEUS	FISH	10	32.8
=	LEEDSICHTHYS	FISH	10	32.8

SHONISAURUS

1 In the 1950s, after numerous remains of these marine lizard were successfully excavated by the Shoshone Mountains in Nevada, USA, its name was created.

Bones of *Pliosaurus* were first discovered in

1841

MOSASAURUS

5 On April 18, 2015, fossil enthusiast Lars Barten and his father Jos discovered the remains of a *Mosasaurus* in the North Brabant region of the Netherlands. *Jurassic World* (2015) features a *Mosasaurus* in a huge water tank.

Pacific Sleeper Sharks live at depths of
6,500 FT

TOP 10

BIGGEST SHARKS

You may have heard of the Great White, but there are even bigger sharks living in our planet's oceans...

	SHARK	LENGTH (M)	(FT)
1	WHALE SHARK	12.7	41.7
2	BASKING SHARK	12.3	40.4
3	GREAT WHITE SHARK	8.0	26.2
4	PACIFIC SLEEPER SHARK	7.4	24.3
=	TIGER SHARK	7.4	24.3
6	GREENLAND SHARK	6.4	21
7	GREAT HAMMERHEAD SHARK	6.1	20
8	THRESHER SHARK	6.0	19.7
9	BLUNTNOSE SIXGILL SHARK	4.8	15.7
10	BIGEYE THRESHER SHARK	4.6	15.1

GREAT HAMMERHEAD SHARK

7 Females of this species (the biggest of the Hammerhead Sharks) can weigh up to 1,280 lb (580.6 kg) when pregnant with a litter of 50+ young.

BLUNTNOSE SIXGILL SHARK

9 This shark's name comes from the fact that most sharks only have five gill slits. This deep-sea shark has been tracked at depths of over 6,150 ft (1874.5 m).

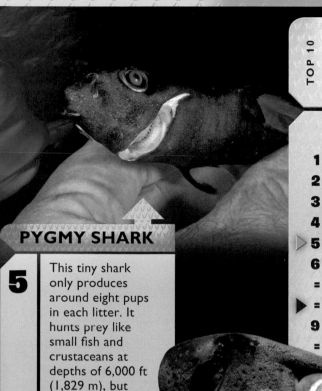

SMALLEST SHARKS

At the opposite end of the shark scale, these sharks are so tiny that none of them exceed the length of a 12 in (30 cm) ruler...

	SHARK	LENGTH (CM)	(IN)
1	DWARF LANTERNSHARK	21.2	8.3
2	PANAMA GHOST CATSHARK	23	9.1
3	PYGMY RIBBONTAIL CATSHARK	24	9.4
4	GREEN LANTERNSHARK	26	10.2
▷ 5	PYGMY SHARK	27	10.6
6	GRANULAR DOGFISH	28	11
=	LOLLIPOP CATSHARK	28	11
▶ =	SPINED PYGMY SHARK	28	11
9	BRISTLY CATSHARK	29	11.4
=	FRINGEFIN LANTERNSHARK	29	11.4

PYGMY SHARK

5 This tiny shark only produces around eight pups in each litter. It hunts prey like small fish and crustaceans at depths of 6,000 ft (1,829 m), but only during the daytime, preferring to stay near the surface at night.

Granular Dogfish have only been caught in waters off the Falkland Islands

GIANT VS TINY

The biggest and smallest sharks side by side...

■ WHALE SHARK
41.7 FT

■ DWARF LANTERNSHARK
8.3 IN

SPINED

6 Like all of the sharks in this top 10, the Spined Pygmy Shark is considered a rare fish that is seldom seen by divers. Its underside is bioluminescent, meaning it glows in the dark.

INTERNATIONAL SPACE STATION

7
The ISS's Expedition 49 (lasting from September to November 2016) comprised of astronauts from Russian, American, and Japanese space agencies, led by Russia's Anatoli Ivanishin.

The Char 2C tank was **13.4** FT tall

TOP 10

BIGGEST VEHICLES OF ALL

By land, sea, sky, and beyond, these are the largest vehicles ever constructed...

	TYPE	NAME	COUNTRY	SIZE (M)	(FT)
1	TRAIN	BHP IRON ORE	AUSTRALIA	7,353	24,124
2	LAND TRANSPORTER	F60 OVERBURDEN CONVEYOR	GERMANY	502.01	1,647
3	SHIP	SEAWISE GIANT OIL TANKER	JAPAN	458.46	1,504.1
4	AIRCRAFT CARRIER	US ENTERPRISE	USA	342	1,122
5	AIRSHIP	HINDENBURG & GRAF ZEPPELIN II	GERMANY	245	803.8
6	SUBMARINE	TYPHOON-CLASS	RUSSIA	175	574.15
▶ 7	SPACE STATION	INTERNATIONAL SPACE STATION	USA/CANADA/RUSSIA/JAPAN/EUROPE	108.5*	356*
8	PLANE	HUGHES H4 HERCULES	USA	97.51**	319.92**
▶ 9	HELICOPTER	MIL V-12	RUSSIA (SOVIET UNION ERA)	37	121.39
10	TANK	CHAR 2C/FCM 2C	FRANCE	10.27	33.69

*All measurements are the vehicles' lengths except: *width and **wingspan.*

MIL V-12

9
Only two prototypes of this, the biggest helicopter ever, have been made. Including its rotor blades, it had a width of 219.816 ft (67 m).

TOP 5 LARGEST

This puts the number one in perspective...

TRAIN
24,124 FT

LAND TRANSPORTER
1,647 FT

SHIP
1,504.1 FT

AIRCRAFT CARRIER
1,122 FT

AIRSHIP
803.8 FT

The hydrofoil craft HMCS *Bras d'Or* was **163.9** FT long

S 2000 SCORPION PEACEKEEPER

9 The top speed of this, the fastest tank in the world, was achieved in Chertsey, UK on March 26, 2002. Repaircraft PLC specialize in renovating and upgrading Scorpion-class tanks.

DPV (DESERT PATROL VEHICLE)

8 These fast and highly manoeuvrable vehicles have been in service since 1991. In the 2007 film *Transformers*, you can see two DPVs helping to move the Allspark.

TOP 10

FASTEST MILITARY VEHICLES EVER

From piloted constructions to unmanned machines, these are the military's speediest vehicles...

	TYPE	NAME	COUNTRY	TOP SPEED (KPH)	(MPH)
1	HYPERSONIC CRUISE VEHICLE	FALCON HTV-2	USA	20,921.47	13,000
2	ROCKET PLANE	NORTH AMERICAN X-15	USA	7,274.24	4,520
3	PLANE	LOCKHEED SR-71 BLACKBIRD	USA	3,529.6	2,193.2
4	UNMANNED AERIAL VEHICLE	BARRACUDA	GERMANY/SPAIN	1,041.3	647
5	HELICOPTER	WESTLAND LYNX	UK	400.87	249.09
6	TRUCK	IFAV (INTERIM FAST ATTACK VEHICLE)	USA	156.11	97
7	SHIP	HMCS BRAS D'OR (FHE 400)	CANADA	117	72
8	LIGHT ATTACK VEHICLE	DPV (DESERT PATROL VEHICLE)	USA	96.56+	60+
9	TANK	S 2000 SCORPION PEACEKEEPER	UK	82.23	51.10
10	SUBMARINE	ALFA CLASS	RUSSIA	74	46

FASTEST MANNED VEHICLES (NON SPACE)

If it requires a human to drive it, it had the chance of
making it into this top 10...

	TYPE	NAME	COUNTRY	TOP SPEED (KPH)	(MPH)
1	ROCKET PLANE	NORTH AMERICAN X-15	USA	7,274.24	4,520
2	PLANE	LOCKHEED SR-71 BLACKBIRD	USA	3,529.6	2,193.2
3	JET-ENGINE CAR	THRUSTSSC	USA	1,227.98	763.04
4	CAR	BLUEBIRD CN7	AUSTRALIA	710	440
5	MOTORCYCLE	TOP 1 OIL-ACK ATTACK	USA	605.7	376.36
6	TRAIN	SCMAGLEV	JAPAN	603.5	375
7	BOAT	SPIRIT OF AUSTRALIA	AUSTRALIA	555.21	345
8	HELICOPTER	EUROCOPTER X3	FRANCE	487.63	303
9	HOVERCRAFT	JENNY II	PORTUGAL	137.4	85.38
10	AIRSHIP	ZEPPELIN LUFTSCHIFFTECHNIK LZ N07-100	GERMANY	112	69.6

BLUEBIRD CN7

4 This is also known as the Proteus-Bluebird Campbell–Norris 7, named after its driver Donald Campbell and sibling designers Lewis and Ken Norris.

1 OIL-ACK ATTA

5 The world's fastest motorcycle has a 1,000 hp (horsepower) capacity, thanks to a Dual 1300cc Suzuki Hayabusa Sport Bike engine paired with an additional Garrett turbo charger.

ThrustSSC's world speed record was set on **OCT 15, 1997**

49

FORD →

6 This motor company gets its name from its founder, American businessman Henry Ford (July 30, 1863 – April 7, 1947). His Ford car firm was founded June 16, 1903 in Michigan, USA.

BMW has made in excess of **2.5 MILLION** cars and motorcycles

VOLKSWAGEN

1 This word means "people's car", and Volkswagen was born out of a need to produce affordable cars for German citizens in the 1920s and 1930s.

TOP 10

HIGHEST GROSSING VEHICULAR COMPANIES

No matter what kind they produce, these are the manufacturers that profit the most from machines...

	COMPANY	HQ'S COUNTRY	REVENUE ($ BILLIONS)
1	VOLKSWAGEN	GERMANY	269
2	TOYOTA	JAPAN	248
3	DAIMLER	GERMANY	172
4	CHINA RAILWAY	CHINA	163
5	GENERAL MOTORS	USA	156
6	FORD	USA	144
7	HONDA	JAPAN	142
8	BMW	GERMANY	106
9	NISSAN MOTOR	JAPAN	103
10	SAIC MOTOR	JAPAN	102

SNOWMOBILE

6 Most high-spec snowmobiles can travel over 150 mph (241 kph). The Lamtrac G-force is the model that achieves more than 210 mph (338 kph).

TOP 10

FASTEST MACHINES IN SPORT

All of the different competitive sports that feature a vehicle have been studied for this chart...

	SPORT	TOP SPEED (KPH)	(MPH)
1	TOP FUEL DRAGSTER	534.59	332.18
2	AIRSHOW STUNT PLANE	426	264.7
3	INDY CAR	413.52	256.95
4	FORMULA ONE CAR	369.9	229.8
5	MOTOR RALLY (NASCAR, ETC)	342.4	212.8
6	SNOWMOBILE	338	210.03
7	POWERBOAT	337.95	210
8	MOTORCYCLE (RACING)	310.99	193.24
9	JETSKI	180.24	112
10	MONSTER TRUCK	159.48	99.1

Early Jetskis were called "Water Scooters" in the **1950s**

GO-KART

Just missing out on a place in the above top 10 is the go-kart. The fastest models can attain speeds of over 80 mph (128.7 kph).

FAST FIVE

Here's how the top 5 compare visually...

TOP FUEL DRAGSTER 332.18 MPH | AIRSHOW STUNT PLANE 264.7 MPH | INDY CAR 256.95 MPH | FORMULA ONE CAR 229.8 MPH | MOTOR RALLY 212.8 MPH

FASTEST PRODUCTION BIKES

If you're a fan of the world of motorcycling, this is the top 10 for you...

	MODEL	TOP SPEED (KPH)	(MPH)
1	DUCATI DESMOSEDICI GP9	348	216.86
2	DUCATI DESMOSEDICI GP4	347.4	215.9
3	DUCATI DESMOSEDICI GP7	337.2	209.6
4	SUZUKI HAYABUSA GSX1300R (1999–2007 MODEL)	312	194
5	MV AGUSTA F4 R 312	310.99	193.24
6	BMW S1000RR	305	190
7	KAWASAKI ZX-12R	301	187
8	KAWASAKI NINJA ZX-14	299.3	186
9	HONDA CBR1100XX SUPER BLACKBIRD	287.3	178.5
10	KAWASAKI NINJA ZX-11	282	175

DUCATI DESMOSEDICI GP

1 What sets this apart from other Ducatis is its carbon fibre chassis. The Cagiva C590 two-stroke 500cc was the first carbon fibre bike to compete at MotoGP, at the 1990 Czech Republic Grand Prix.

Honda CBR1100XX Super Blackbird fuel capacity: **6.1** GALLONS

BMW S1000RR

6 Although now available for any bike fan to own, this model was initially created for the the 2009 Superbike World Championship (founded in 1988).

9ff GT9-R is
15.53 FT
long

FASTEST **CARS**

This combines production cars and concept ones to create a top 10 of the speediest cars...

	MODEL	TOP SPEED (KPH)	(MPH)
1	HENNESSEY VENOM GT	435.31	270.49
2	BUGATTI VEYRON 16.4 SUPER SPORT	431.07	269.86
3	KOENIGSEGG AGERA	418.42	260
4	SSC ULTIMATE AERO	414.31	257.44
5	9FF GT9-R	413.59	257
6	BUGATTI VEYRON GRAND SPORT VITESSE	408.84	254.04
7	SALEEN S7 TWIN-TURBO	399.11	248
8	KOENIGSEGG CCX	394.28	245
9	MCLAREN F1	391.06	243
10	KOENIGSEGG CCR	387.87	241.01

SALEEN S7 TWIN-TURBO

7 Its twin turbos boost its power to 750 hp (horsepower). This car gets its name from Steve Saleen's namesake company. Since 1983 it has specialized in high-spec sports cars.

HENNESSEY VENOM GT

1 Models have been produced since 2011. Its record-setting speed was achieved at the space shuttle landing strip at Florida, USA's Kennedy Space Center on February 14, 2014.

53

OHIO

2 This class of submarine can travel up to 23 mph (37 kph) under the waves. It is the largest sub constructed for the US Navy.

Number of Ohio-class submarines owned by the US Navy:

18

TOP 10

LONGEST SUBMARINES

These submersible military vehicles cost millions of dollars to develop and construct...

	CLASS	COUNTRY	LENGTH (M)	(FT)
1	TYPHOON	RUSSIA	175	574.14
2	BOREI	RUSSIA	170	557.74
=	OHIO	USA	170	557.74
4	DELTA III	RUSSIA	166	544.62
5	OSCAR II	RUSSIA	155	508.53
6	VANGUARD	UK	149.9	491.8
7	TRIOMPHANT	FRANCE	138	452.76
8	YASEN	RUSSIA	120	393.7
9	VIRGINIA	USA	115	377.3
10	SIERRA II	RUSSIA	111	364.17

TRIOMPHANT

7 There are four active submarines in this class currently serving the French Navy. Each holds 96 sailors and 15 officers.

OCEANIC EXPLORATION

USA

1 Founded on October 13, 1775, the US Navy is the largest navy on Earth. Including reserves, it has almost 450,000 personnel and nearly 4,000 aircraft.

The largest aircraft carriers can hold **90** aircraft

ORIGINS OF THE AIRCRAFT CARRIER

During the 1910s, the US Navy and British Royal Navy began developing ways to have aircraft take off and land from a vessel. In 1918, the latter's HMS *Argus* became the first official aircraft carrier.

MOST AIRCRAFT CARRIERS

TOP 10

Hundreds of billions of dollars have been spent designing and constructing these metallic titans...

	COUNTRY	NUMBER IN SERVICE	TOTAL NUMBER EVER BUILT
1	USA	10	68
2	UK	0	40
3	JAPAN	0	20
4	FRANCE	1	8
5	RUSSIA	1	7
6	INDIA	2	3
7	SPAIN	1	3
8	AUSTRALIA	0	3
=	CANADA	0	3
10	ITALY	2	2

AIRCRAFT NATIONS

These 5 countries have constructed the most...

USA 68
UK 40
JAPAN 20
FRANCE 8
RUSSIA 7

The guessing game "Battleship" echoes the US board game "Baslinda," dating from **1890**

GLOIRE

1 This French vessel had 4.5-in (11.4-cm) thick iron plating, which covered a bulky timber construction. It was built with 36 guns.

MODERN BATTLESHIPS

This approach to naval warfare is now a thing of the past. The British Royal Navy's HMS *Vanguard* was one of the last in use. It was decommissioned in1960.

TOP 10

FIRST CLASSES OF IRONCLAD BATTLESHIP

Once the all-wooden ships got superseded by metal, these were the original classes...

	CLASS	YEAR OF LAUNCH
1	GLOIRE	1859
2	WARRIOR	1860
3	MAGENTA	1861
=	TERRIBLE	1861
5	PROVENCE	1863
=	PRINCIPE DI CARIGNANO	1863
=	RE D'ITALIA	1863
=	REGINA MARIA PIA	1863
9	PERVENETS	1864
10	ROMA	1865

FORCES OF NATURE

ZONE **3**

TOP 10

BIGGEST COUNTRIES
(LAND MASS)

Of the 196 countries there are on our planet, these are the 10 largest...

	COUNTRY	SIZE (KM²)	(MI²)
1	RUSSIA	17,098,242	6,601,668
2	CANADA	9,984,670	3,855,100
3	CHINA	9,706,961	3,747,879
4	USA	9,629,091	3,705,407
5	BRAZIL	8,514,877	3,287,612
6	AUSTRALIA	7,692,024	2,969,907
7	INDIA	3,166,414	1,222,559
8	ARGENTINA	2,780,400	1,073,500
9	KAZAKHSTAN	2,724,900	1,052,100
10	ALGERIA	2,381,741	919,595

INDIA

7 The most popular sport in India is cricket. The national team played its first Test match in 1932, but its first team was established in 1792.

Monaco, the second smallest country in the world, covers just

0.78 MI²

AUSTRALIA

6 This country's name comes from the Latin for "southern land", *Terra Australis*. Tourism contributes approximately $100 million a day to its economy.

NORWAY

7 90 per cent of Norway is mountainous, with a total of 291 peaks. Galdhøpiggen in Jotunheimen is the tallest at 8,100 ft (2,469 m).

RUSSIA

3 Nearly 30 million tourists visit Russia each year. St Petersburg, established in 1703 by Peter Alexeyevich (aka Peter the Great), is the most popular place to visit.

TOP 10

LONGEST COASTLINES
These countries are connected to the oceans of the world more than any others...

	COUNTRY	LENGTH OF COASTLINE (KM)	(MI)
1	CANADA	265,523	164,988.34
2	USA	133,312	82,836.24
3	RUSSIA	110,310	68,543.46
4	INDONESIA	95,181	59,142.73
5	CHILE	78,563	48,816.78
6	AUSTRALIA	66,530	41,339.83
7	NORWAY	53,199	33,056.33
8	PHILIPPINES	33,900	21,064.48
9	BRAZIL	33,379	20,740.75
10	FINLAND	31,119	19,336.45

CANADA

1 Canada celebrates its original inhabitants, Canadian Aboriginals, and the history of the country on National Aboriginal Day, June 21. 4.4 per cent of Canada's population are Aboriginals.

USA's population is **325.9 MILLION**

COASTLINE LENGTHS
This graph shows the 5 longest coastlines...

CANADA 164,988.34 MI USA 82,836.24 MI RUSSIA 68,543.46 MI INDONESIA 59,142.73 MI CHILE 48,816.78 MI

1ST VS. 10TH

La Paz vs. Kabul: elevation above sea level...

LA PAZ **11,942 FT**

KABUL **5,873 FT**

QUITO

2 Founded in 1534, Quito is now home to nearly 3 million people. It has seven museums and also seven professional soccer teams.

TOP 10

HIGHEST CAPITAL CITIES

Even the city at tenth place in this list is located more than a mile above sea level...

	NAME	COUNTRY	ELEVATION ABOVE SEA LEVEL (M)	(FT)
1	LA PAZ	BOLIVIA	3,640	11,942
2	QUITO	ECUADOR	2,850	9,350
3	THIMPHU	BHUTAN	2,648	8,688
4	BOGOTÁ	COLOMBIA	2,625	8,612
5	ADDIS ABABA	ETHIOPIA	2,355	7,726
6	ASMARA	ERITREA	2,325	7,628
7	SANA'A	YEMEN	2,250	7,382
8	MEXICO CITY	MEXICO	2,240	7,350
9	NAIROBI	KENYA	1,795	5,889
10	KABUL	AFGHANISTAN	1,790	5,873

Nairobi covers

269 MI²

ADDIS ABABA

5 This Ethiopian city is home to a childcare centre called We Are The Future. The centre is dedicated to improving the lives and well-being of children of Addis Ababa.

Lake Assal is **130** FT deep

BADWATER BASIN

9 Natural salt at Badwater Basin, in California, is subject to repeated freezing, thawing and evaporating. Tourists visit the site to see the unusual hexagonal salt shapes strewn across the basin.

DEAD SEA

1 This sea is called 'Dead' since the water is devoid of all life except bacteria and fungi. The Dead Sea is nine times saltier than the ocean, and 997 ft (304 m) deep.

TOP 10

COUNTRIES WITH THE LOWEST POINTS OF ELEVATION

In contrast with the list opposite, these locations are at extraordinary low points...

	PLACE	COUNTRY/COUNTRIES	LOWEST POINT BELOW SEA LEVEL (M)	(FT)
1	DEAD SEA	ISRAEL, JORDAN, PALESTINE	-428	-1,402
2	SEA OF GALILEE	ISRAEL	-214	-702
3	LAKE ASSAL	DJIBOUTI	-155	-509
4	AYDINGKOL	CHINA	-154	-505
5	QATTARA DEPRESSION	EGYPT	-133	-436
6	KARAGIYE DEPRESSION	KAZAKHSTAN	-132	-433
7	DANAKIL DEPRESSION	ETHIOPIA	-125	-410
8	LAGUNA DEL CARBÓN	ARGENTINA	-105	-344
9	BADWATER BASIN	USA	-85	-279
10	VPADINA AKCHANAYA	TURKMENISTAN	-81	-266

OCEANS VS. SEAS

The water areas compared...

- OCEAN **151,423,000** MI²
- SEAS **7,460,000** MI²

The Indian Ocean can reach

82 °F

LARGEST OCEANS & SEAS

TOP 10

Earth is often called the Blue Planet as 71 per cent of its surface is covered in water...

	NAME	TYPE	AREA (KM²)	(MI²)
1	PACIFIC	OCEAN	166,266,876	64,196,000
2	ATLANTIC	OCEAN	86,505,602	33,400,000
3	INDIAN	OCEAN	73,555,662	28,400,000
4	SOUTHERN	OCEAN	52,646,688	20,327,000
5	ARCTIC	OCEAN	13,208,939	5,100,000
6	PHILIPPINE	SEA	5,179,976	2,000,000
7	CORAL	SEA	4,791,478	1,850,000
8	ARABIAN	SEA	3,861,672	1,491,000
9	SOUTH CHINA	SEA	2,973,306	1,148,000
10	CARIBBEAN	SEA	2,514,878	971,000

ARCTIC WILDLIFE

A broad range of wildlife, including the walrus, narwal, beluga, snowy owl, polar bear, caribou and lemming thrive in the subzero temperatures of the Arctic region.

BERMUDA TRIANGLE MYSTERY

The area of the ocean between Bermuda, the state of Florida, and Puerto Rico is popularly known as the Devil's Triangle. Planes, ships and their unlucky passengers, have disappeared here without a trace.

CASPIAN SEA

1 This body of water is where the largest freshwater fish in the world lives. The Beluga Sturgeon can reach 24 ft (7.3 m) in length. It is critically endangered due to overfishing.

TOP 10

LARGEST LAKES

If you live near a lake, it is one of an estimated 117 million on this planet...

	NAME	LOCATION	AREA (KM²)	(MI²)
1	CASPIAN SEA	IRAN, RUSSIA, TURKMENISTAN, KAZAKHSTAN, AZERBAIJAN	371,000	143,000
2	SUPERIOR	CANADA, USA	82,414	31,820
3	VICTORIA	UGANDA, KENYA, TANZANIA	69,485	26,828
4	HURON	CANADA, USA	59,600	23,000
5	MICHIGAN	USA	58,000	22,000
6	TANGANYIKA	TANZANIA, DEMOCRATIC REPUBLIC OF THE CONGO, BURUNDI, ZAMBIA	32,893	12,700
7	BAIKAL	RUSSIA	31,500	12,200
8	GREAT BEAR	CANADA	31,080	12,000
9	MALAWI	MOZAMBIQUE, TANZANIA, MALAWI	30,044	11,600
10	GREAT SLAVE	CANADA	28,930	11,170

SUPERIOR

2 Lake Superior, one of the five Great Lakes, reaches 1,333 ft (406.3 m) deep. Over the centuries, sightings of a huge, serpent-type creature called Pressie, have been recorded here.

The Caspian Sea is home to

31

islands

YARLUNG TSANGPO GRAND CANYON

1 This is one of the rare places on Earth that hasn't been extensively explored and affected by humankind. It's so vast that it experiences arctic and sub-tropical temperatures.

TOP 10

DEEPEST CANYONS

To put these measurements into context, the number one entry is almost four miles deep...

	NAME	LOCATION	DEEPEST POINT (M)	(FT)
1	YARLUNG TSANGPO GRAND CANYON	TIBET	6,009	19,714.6
2	THE KALI GANDAKI GORGE	NEPAL	5,571	18,277.6
3	INDUS GORGE	PAKISTAN	5,200	17,060.4
4	COLCA CANYON	PERU	4,160	13,648.3
5	TIGER LEAPING GORGE	CHINA	3,790	12,434.4
6	COTAHUASI CANYON	PERU	3,535	11,597.8
7	URIQUE CANYON (ONE OF THE 6 COPPER CANYONS)	MEXICO	1,879	6,164.7
8	THE GRAND CANYON	USA	1,828	5,997.4
9	BLYDE RIVER CANYON	SOUTH AFRICA	1,383	4,537.4
10	TARA RIVER CANYON	MONTENEGRO	1,300	4,265.1

Tibet's Yarlung Tsangpo Grand Canyon is

150 MI
long

PERU CANYONS

This is how the featured Peruvian canyons compare...

COLCA CANYON
13,648.3 FT

COTAHUASI CANYON
11,597.8 FT

YANGTZE

3 This river has 700 tributaries. One of its dams, the Three Gorges Dam, is the largest power station in the world. It took 14 years to complete.

CONGO

9 There are 686 species of fish (that we know of) in the Congo River, including the air-breathing lungfish. 80 per cent of this river's species exist only there.

TOP 10

LONGEST RIVERS

These 10 rivers from all over the world total more than 35,000 miles in length...

	NAME	OUTFLOW	LENGTH (KM)	(MI)
1	AMAZON – UCAYALI – APURÍMAC	ATLANTIC OCEAN	6,992	4,345
2	NILE – KAGERA	MEDITERRANEAN	6,853	4,258
3	YANGTZE	EAST CHINA SEA	6,300	3,917
4	MISSISSIPPI – MISSOURI – JEFFERSON	GULF OF MEXICO	6,275	3,902
5	YENISEI – ANGARA – SELENGE	KARA SEA	5,539	3,445
6	HUANG HE	BOHAI SEA	5,464	3,395
7	OB – IRTYSH	GULF OF OB	5,410	3,364
8	PARANÁ – RÍO DE LA PLATA	RÍO DE LA PLATA	4,880	3,030
9	CONGO – CHAMBESHI	ATLANTIC OCEAN	4,700	2,922
10	AMUR – ARGUN	SEA OF OKHOTSK	4,444	2,763

AMAZON

1 The Amazon River flows through four countries, stretching almost the entire width of their combined land mass. During the wet season, it reaches 30 miles (48.2 km) wide.

The Amazon River sees

1,584 MI³

water flow through it each year

LAYA

10 The indigenous inhabitants of Laya are known as the Layap. They wear a distinctive, cone-shaped hat made of treated bamboo.

Bolivia's population is approx. **10 MILLION**

COMPARING THE HIGHEST

Here is a graphic expression of this chart's top 5...

LA RINCONADA 16,728 FT	WENQUAN 15,980 FT	KORZOK 15,000 FT	PARINACOTA 14,435 FT	DOLPA 14,301 FT

TOP 10

HIGHEST RESIDENTIAL PLACES ABOVE SEA LEVEL

Although not literally the tallest points on Earth, these are the highest places that people live...

	PLACE	COUNTRY	ELEVATION ABOVE SEA LEVEL (M)	(FT)
1	LA RINCONADA	PERU	5,100	16,728
2	WENQUAN	CHINA	4,870	15,980
3	KORZOK	INDIA	4,570	15,000
4	PARINACOTA	CHILE	4,400	14,435
5	DOLPA	NEPAL	4,360	14,301
6	MINA PIRQUITAS	ARGENTINA	4,340	14,240
7	COLQUECHACA	BOLIVIA	4,170	13,680
8	QARABOLAQ	AFGHANISTAN	4,139	13,579
9	CHATYNDY	KYRGYZSTAN	4,013	13,166
10	LAYA	BHUTAN	3,820	12,533

LA RINCONADA

1 A colossal glacier called La Bella Durmiente (which translates as "The Sleeping Beauty") sits by this Peruvian city, which has a population of 50,000.

DEEPEST REALMS

With depths ranging between five and six miles, these are the lowest known points on Earth...

	NAME	LOCATION	DEEPEST POINT BELOW SEA LEVEL (M)	(FT)
1	MARIANA TRENCH	PACIFIC OCEAN	11,033	36,197.5
2	TONGA TRENCH	PACIFIC OCEAN	10,882	35,702.1
3	JAPAN TRENCH	PACIFIC OCEAN	10,544	34,593.2
4	PHILIPPINE TRENCH	PACIFIC OCEAN	10,540	34,580
5	KURIL-KAMCHATKA TRENCH	PACIFIC OCEAN	10,500	34,448.8
6	KERMADEC TRENCH	PACIFIC OCEAN	10,047	32,962.6
7	IZU-OGASAWARA TRENCH	PACIFIC OCEAN	9,780	32,086.6
8	PUERTO RICO TRENCH	ATLANTIC OCEAN	8,648	28,372.7
9	SOUTH SANDWICH TRENCH	ATLANTIC OCEAN	8,428	27,650.9
10	ATACAMA TRENCH	PACIFIC OCEAN	8,065	26,460

Just off the chart, the Atlantic Ocean's Romanche Trench is **25,459.3 FT** deep

TONGA TRENCH

2 When the Apollo 13 space mission failed, its Lunar Module's re-entry was coerced to splash down and sink into the Tonga Trench. This is because it contained an RTG (Radioisotope Thermoelectric Generator) of radioactive plutonium.

THE MARIANA TRENCH CHALLENGE

Canadian filmmaker James Cameron made history when he piloted the *Deepsea Challenger* to the bottom of the Mariana Trench on March 26, 2012.

ANDES

3 The highest point along the Andes is Aconcagua. Its maximum elevation is 22,837 ft (6,960.8 m).

German explorer Paul Güssfeldt was the first European to attempt to climb Aconcagua in **1883**

TOP 10

LONGEST MOUNTAIN RANGES

You may be familiar with the names of mountain ranges above water, but the biggest are beneath the waves...

	RANGE	MOUNTAIN TYPE	LOCATION	LENGTH (KM)	(MI)
1	MID-OCEANIC RIDGE	OCEANIC	(GLOBAL)	65,000	40,389
2	MID-ATLANTIC RIDGE	OCEANIC	ATLANTIC OCEAN	10,000	6,214
3	ANDES	LAND	SOUTH AMERICA	7,000	4,350
4	ROCKIES	LAND	NORTH AMERICA	4,800	2,983
5	TRANSANTARCTIC	LAND	ANTARCTICA	3,542	2,201
6	GREAT DIVIDING RANGE	LAND	AUSTRALIA	3,059	1,901
7	HIMALAYAS	LAND	ASIA	2,576	1,601
8	SOUTHEAST INDIAN RIDGE	OCEANIC	INDIAN OCEAN	2,300	1,429
9	SOUTHWEST INDIAN RIDGE	OCEANIC	RODRIGUEZ ISLAND TO PRINCE EDWARD ISLANDS	1,931	1,200
10	PACIFIC-ANTARCTIC RIDGE	OCEANIC	SOUTH PACIFIC OCEAN	1,029	639

MID-OCEANIC RIDGE

1 The complete system of mid-oceanic ridges that exists in every ocean on the planet is known as the Ocean Ridge. It is almost 10 times the length of the Andes.

MID-ATLANTIC RIDGE

2 Some scientists believe the MAR (Mid-Atlantic Ridge) was formed when the original "super-continent" of Pangea began to break apart 180 million years ago.

TUGELA FALLS

2 This system of five drops does not fall as one cascade of water. In cold periods, the higher falls freeze into icy columns. It is considered best to view the falls after rainfall.

ANGEL FALLS

1 Of its two drops, the longest is 2,648 ft (807 m). The falls drop into Venezuela's Canaima National Park, which is a UNESCO (United Nations Educational, Scientific, and Cultural Organization) World Heritage Site.

Vinnufossen is the tallest waterfall in Europe and has **4** drops

HIGHEST WATERFALLS

Have you ever visited one of the most famous waterfalls in the world? Compare its height with these...

	NAME	LOCATION	HEIGHT (M)	(FT)
1	ANGEL FALLS	BOLÍVAR STATE (VENEZUELA)	979	3,212
2	TUGELA FALLS	KWAZULU-NATAL (SOUTH AFRICA)	948	3,110
3	CATARATAS LAS TRES HERMANAS	AYACUCHO (PERU)	914	3,000
4	OLO'UPENA FALLS	MOLOKAI, HAWAII (USA)	900	2,953
5	CATARATA YUMBILLA	AMAZONAS (PERU)	896	2,940
6	VINNUFOSSEN	MØRE OG ROMSDAL (NORWAY)	860	2,822
7	BALÅIFOSSEN	HORDALAND (NORWAY)	850	2,788
8	PU'UKA'OKU FALLS	MOLOKAI, HAWAII (USA)	840	2,756
=	JAMES BRUCE FALLS	BRITISH COLUMBIA (CANADA)	840	2,756
10	BROWNE FALLS	SOUTH ISLAND (NEW ZEALAND)	836	2,743

Kuwait International Airport serves over

9 MILLION passengers each year

KEBILI

2

As well as being one of the hottest places on this planet, amazingly, Kebili has evidence that points to human habitation near the town dating back 200,000 years.

DEATH VALLEY

1

The Native American tribe of the Timbisha have been living in Death Valley for over a thousand years.

TOP 10

HOTTEST PLACES

Cells in the human body start to die at around 113ºF (45ºC), so these are dangerous air temperatures...

	LOCATION	DATE	TEMPERATURE (ºC)	(ºF)
1	DEATH VALLEY, CALIFORNIA (USA)	JUL 10, 1913	56.7	134
2	KEBILI (TUNISIA)	JUL 7, 1931	55	131
3	TIRAT ZVI (ISRAEL)	JUN 21, 1942	54	129
4	SULAIBYA (KUWAIT)	JUL 31, 2012	53.6	128.5
5	KUWAIT INTERNATIONAL AIRPORT (KUWAIT)	AUG 3, 2011	53.5	128.3
=	MOHENJO-DARO, SINDH (PAKISTAN)	MAY 26, 2010	53.5	128.3
7	NASIRIYAH, ALI AIR BASE (IRAQ)	AUG 3, 2011	53	127.4
8	BASRA, IRAQ	JUN 14, 2010	52	125.6
=	SAN LUIS RÍO COLORADO (MEXICO)	JUL 6, 1966	52	125.6
=	JEDDAH (SAUDI ARABIA)	JUN 22, 2010	52	125.6

TOP 10

COLDEST PLACES

Pure water freezes at 32°F (0°C), which highlights just how cold these realms are...

	LOCATION	DATE	TEMPERATURE (°C)	(°F)
1	VOSTOK STATION (ANTARCTICA)	JUL 21, 1983	-89.2	-128.6
2	AMUNDSEN-SCOTT SOUTH POLE STATION (SOUTH POLE)	JUN 23, 1982	-82.8	-117
3	DOME A (EAST ANTARCTICA)	JUL 5, 2007	-82.5	-116.5
4	VERKHOYANSK & OYMYAKON SAKHA REPUBLIC (RUSSIA)	FEB 6, 1933	-68	-90
5	NORTH ICE (GREENLAND)	JAN 9, 1954	-66.1	-87
6	SNAG, YUKON (CANADA)	FEB 3, 1947	-63	-81
7	PROSPECT CREEK, ALASKA (USA)	JAN 23, 1971	-62	-80
8	UST-SHCHUGER (RUSSIA)	DEC 31, 1978	-58.1	-72.6
9	MALGOVIK, VÄSTERBOTTEN (SWEDEN)	DEC 13, 1941	-53	-63.4
10	MOHE COUNTY (CHINA)	FEB 13, 1969	-52.3	-62.1

VERKHOYANSK & OYMYAKON SAKHA REPUBLIC

4 It may be one of the coldest places on Earth, but March 2014 saw a deep-dive investigation into the region's Labynkyr Lake. Reported sightings of an unknown creature in the lake date back centuries.

AMUNDSEN-SCOTT SOUTH POLE STATION

2 The original version of this station was built in 1956. Nowadays, ongoing research of the galaxy is conducted there with the 32.8-ft (10-m) diameter South Pole Telescope.

Antarctica has **0** permanent residents

FAR BELOW FREEZING

Here is how the top 5 coldest places compare...

ANTARCTICA -128.6°F	SOUTH POLE -117°F	EAST ANTARCTICA -116.5°F	RUSSIA -90°F	GREENLAND -87°F

MOUNT ONTAKE

3 With a height of 10,062 ft (3,067 m), this is the second tallest volcano in Japan. The biggest is Mount Fuji, at 12,388 ft (3,776 m).

MOUNT MERAPI

1 Appropriate for a volcano, Mount Merapi translates to mean "Fire Mountain". Scientific analysis puts Merapi at around 400,000 years old.

TOP 10

MOST RECENT & DEADLIEST VOLCANIC ERUPTIONS

They may be ancient, but many volcanoes remain active with the potential to devastate their surroundings...

WHAT IS "VEI"

The Volcanic Explosivity Index provides a way to measure the impact of a volcanic eruption. The 1–8 scale measures the volume of volcanic material that is discharged.

	NAME	LOCATION	YEAR	VEI	KNOWN FATALITIES
1	MOUNT MERAPI	INDONESIA	2010	4	353
2	NYIRAGONGO	DR CONGO	2002	1	147
3	MOUNT ONTAKE	JAPAN	2014	3	61
4	NABRO	ERITREA	2011	4	38
5	MOUNT SINABUNG	INDONESIA	2014	2	15
6	KELUD	INDONESIA	2014	4	2
7	CHAITÉN	CHILE	2008	4	1
8	CALBUCO	CHILE	2015	4	0
9	PUYEHUE-CORDÓN CAULLE	CHILE	2011	5	0
10	GRÍMSVÖTN	ICELAND	2011	4	0

Chile was the location of the

33

miners who were successfully rescued on Oct 13, 2010

BIGGEST EARTHQUAKES

Minor earthquakes occur unnoticed all over the world every day, but others are extremely deadly...

	LOCATION	DATE	MAGNITUDE (RICHTER SCALE)
1	VALDIVIA (CHILE)	MAY 22, 1960	9.5
2	ALASKA (USA)	MAR 27, 1964	9.2
3	SUMATRA (INDONESIA)	DEC 26, 2004	9.1–9.3
4	TŌHOKU REGION (JAPAN)	MAR 11, 2011	9.0
=	KAMCHATKA (RUSSIA)	NOV 4, 1952	9.0
6	SUMATRA (INDONESIA)	NOV 25, 1833	8.8–9.2
7	ECUADOR (COLOMBIA)	JAN 31, 1906	8.8
=	MAULE (CHILE)	FEB 27, 2010	8.8
=	ARICA (CHILE)	SEP 16, 1615	8.8
10	KRAKATOA (INDONESIA)	AUG 26, 1883	8.75

TŌHOKU REGION

4 In addition to the 2011 quake, there was also one in 2006 that killed approximately 5,000 people. Nearly a quarter of a million people were also rendered homeless through fear of a full-blown volcanic eruption.

Indonesia has
150
active volcanoes

SUMATRA

3 Sumatra's landscape features several volcanoes. North Sumatra's most populated city is Medan, with 2.1 million residents.

Haiti covers
10,714 MI²

SPIRIT LAKE

2 When Mount St. Helens erupted, Spirit Lake was struck with the full force. Now, this strange "raft" of more than a million trees felled from the blast can still be seen.

TALLEST TSUNAMIS

TOP 10

Any significant natural or man-made disturbance of a large area of water can cause a seismic sea wave...

	LOCATION	YEAR	HEIGHT OF TSUNAMI (FT)	(M)
1	LITUYA BAY, ALASKA	1958	1,719	524
2	SPIRIT LAKE, WASHINGTON	1980	853	260
3	VAJONT DAM, ITALY	1963	820	250
4	MOUNT UNZEN, KYUSHU, JAPAN	1792	328	100
5	ISHIGAKI & MIYAKOJIMA ISLANDS, JAPAN	1771	262	79.9
6	INDIAN OCEAN, SOUTH ASIA	2004	98.4	30
7	LISBON, PORTUGAL	1755	66	20.1
8	MESSINA, ITALY	1908	40	12.2
9	HOEI, JAPAN	1707	32	9.8
10	MEIJI-SANRIKU, JAPAN	1896	30	9.1

VAJONT DAM

3 A reminder of how engineering and research can go wrong: on October 9, 1963, a landslide triggered an immense wave over the top of this dam, killing thousands.

ERAS COMPARED

Here's how the number of tsunamis in the chart compare by century...

21ST	20TH	19TH	18TH
1	4	1	4

TOP 10

DEADLIEST FLOODS

As much as water is needed for all life on this planet, it can fast become a cruel, unpredictable enemy...

	RIVER (COUNTRY)	YEAR	FATALITIES
1	YANGTZE, HUANG HE (CHINA)	1931	**2.5–3.7 MILLION**
2	HUANG HE (CHINA)	1887	**900,000–2 MILLION**
3	HUANG HE CHINA)	1938	**500,000–700,000**
4	INDIAN OCEAN TSUNAMI (SEVERAL)	2004	**230,000–310,000**
5	BANQIAO DAM FAILURE/TYPHOON NINA (CHINA)	1975	**231,000**
6	YANGTZE (CHINA)	1935	**145,000**
7	MESSINA EARTHQUAKE & TSUNAMI (ITALY)	1908	**123,000**
8	ST FELIX'S FLOOD (NETHERLANDS)	1530	**100,000+**
9	HANOI & RED RIVER DELTA FLOODS (N. VIETNAM)	1971	**100,000**
=	LISBON EARTHQUAKE & TSUNAMI (PORTUGAL)	1755	**100,000**

ST FELIX'S FLOOD

8 The day of this flood became known as Evil Saturday. Without a series of dikes, much of the Netherlands would be underwater. The country was made into a plain by sediment formed over millennia of floods.

Huang He is
3,395 MI
long

INDIAN OCEAN TSUNAMI

4 A 9.1 earthquake led to the catastrophic tsunami of 2004. It was so powerful, it caused earthquakes in Alaska. There were 25,120 earthquakes (all magnitudes) in 2004.

TSUNAMI EVACUATION ROUTE

VIDEO GAMES

ZONE 4

BIGGEST-SELLING GAMING CONSOLES/PLATFORMS

Examining sales from every gaming system, these are the kings of sales figures...

	PLATFORM	MADE BY	RELEASED	UNIT SALES (MILLIONS)
1	PLAYSTATION 2	SONY	2000	157.68
2	NINTENDO DS	NINTENDO	2004	154.88
3	GAME BOY/GAME BOY COLOR	NINTENDO	1989/1998	118.69
4	PLAYSTATION	SONY	1994	104.25
5	WII	NINTENDO	2006	101.18
6	PLAYSTATION 3	SONY	2006	86.08
7	XBOX 360	MICROSOFT	2005	85.06
8	GAME BOY ADVANCE	NINTENDO	2001	81.51
9	PLAYSTATION PORTABLE	SONY	2004	80.82
10	NINTENDO ENTERTAINMENT SYSTEM	NINTENDO	1983	61.91

GAME BOY

3

Before the colour version came along in 1998, the original Game Boy had reigned the handheld gaming world since 1989. Manufacturing of both platforms ceased in 2003.

PS2 has sold the most units of games of any console:
1,661.95 MILLION

PS4 & XBOX ONE SALES

Both released in November 2013, Sony's PS4 has sold 36.1 million units, whereas Microsoft's game system has only shifted 19.5 million. The PS4 has seen game sales of 206.8 million units, with Xbox One trailing behind with 112.8 million.

GAMING BY ERA

Here is how the platforms' successes compares by the decades...

- 80s **2**
- 90s **1**
- 00s **7**

10 The Nintendo Wii was so popular in 2007 that manufacturing could not keep up with public demand for the console. More than 958 million units of Wii games have been sold.

NINTENDO ENTERTAINMENT SYSTEM

1 The NES was released on July 15, 1983. The basic set (just the console, no games) cost $89.99. A deluxe set with the ROB (Robotic Operating Buddy) peripheral retailed for $199.99.

Microsoft's original Xbox was in production for

7.3 years

LONGEST-RUNNING PLATFORMS

From the date they were first released, to when manufacturing stopped, these are the gaming systems that have stuck around the longest...

	PLATFORM	MADE BY	YEARS IN PRODUCTION	TOTAL YEARS
1	NINTENDO ENTERTAINMENT SYSTEM	NINTENDO	1983–2003	20
2	GAME BOY/GAME BOY COLOR	NINTENDO	1989–2003	14
3	PLAYSTATION	SONY	1994–2006	12
=	PLAYSTATION 2	SONY	2000–12	12
=	NINTENDO DS/3DS/3DSI XL	NINTENDO	2004–PRESENT	12
6	XBOX 360	MICROSOFT	2005–PRESENT	11
7	PLAYSTATION 3	SONY	2006–PRESENT	10
=	PLAYSTATION PORTABLE	SONY	2004–14	10
=	SUPER NINTENDO ENTERTAINMENT SYSTEM	NINTENDO	1993–2003	10
▶10	WII	NINTENDO	2006–13	7

BIGGEST-SELLING HANDHELD CONSOLES/PLATFORMS

Gaming has been a popular portable pastime for decades, and these are the biggest successes...

	PLATFORM	MADE BY	RELEASED	UNIT SALES (MILLIONS)
1	NINTENDO DS	NINTENDO	2004	**154.88**
2	GAME BOY/GAME BOY COLOR	NINTENDO	1989/1998	**118.69**
3	GAME BOY ADVANCE	NINTENDO	2001	**81.51**
4	PLAYSTATION PORTABLE	SONY	2004	**80.82**
5	NINTENDO 3DS	NINTENDO	2011	**55.27**
6	PLAYSTATION VITA	SONY	2011	**12.86**
7	GAME GEAR	SEGA	1990	**10.62**
8	LEAPSTER	LEAPFROG ENTERPRISES	2008	**4**
9	NEO GEO POCKET/POCKET COLOR	SNK	1998/1999	**2**
10	TURBOEXPRESS	NEC	1990	**1.5**

PLAYSTATION VITA

6 52.8 million units of games have been sold for this Sony handheld console. In comparison, Nintendo's Game Boy saw 501.1 million games sold.

Sega's colour handheld, the Game Gear, was released on **OCT 6, 1990**

NINTENDO 3DS

5 Nintendo's 3DS XL (with a 90 per cent bigger screen) launched in July 2012. More than 229 million copies of games for the 3DS have been sold worldwide.

The *Animal Crossing* franchise has shifted

29.88 MILLION units

POKÉMON X/Y

1 Released on October 12, 2013, Pokémon X/Y saw 70 new species of Pokémon for players to train. The game also saw the ability to evolve characters into new forms.

SUPER SMASH BROS.

7 *Super Smash Bros. For Wii U And 3DS* is the fifth title in the franchise, which debuted in 1999 on the N64. The brand has shifted more than 37 million units worldwide.

TOP 10

BIGGEST-SELLING 3DS GAMES

Nintendo's handheld continues to sell in the millions, and these are its most popular games...

	NAME	GENRE	RELEASED	UNIT SALES (MILLIONS)
1	POKÉMON X/Y	RPG	2013	**13.17**
2	MARIO KART 7	RACING	2011	**11.13**
3	SUPER MARIO 3D LAND	PLATFORM	2011	**10.37**
4	POKÉMON OMEGA RUBY/ ALPHA SAPPHIRE	RPG	2014	**9.07**
5	NEW SUPER MARIO BROS. 2	PLATFORM	2012	**9.01**
6	ANIMAL CROSSING: NEW LEAF	ACTION	2012	**8.25**
7	SUPER SMASH BROS. FOR WII U AND 3DS	FIGHTING	2014	**6.6**
8	TOMODACHI LIFE	SIMULATION	2013	**4.45**
9	LUIGI'S MANSION: DARK MOON	ADVENTURE	2013	**4.33**
10	THE LEGEND OF ZELDA: OCARINA OF TIME	ACTION	2011	**3.82**

The Legend Of Zelda: The Wind Waker is the

10TH

Zelda game

SUPER MARIO 3D WORLD

5 Rosalina watches over the cosmos and is a playable character once World 2 of Super Mario 3D World has been completed.

SPLATOON

6 A brand new game title, Splatoon features humanoid creatures that can take on the form of squid. Players' challenges include rescuing the Great Zapfish.

TOP 10

BIGGEST WII U GAMES

Since the Wii U was first released on November 18, 2012, these games have been the big sellers...

	NAME	GENRE	RELEASED	UNIT SALES (MILLIONS)
1	MARIO KART 8	RACING	2014	5.43
2	NEW SUPER MARIO BROS. U	ACTION	2012	4.89
3	NINTENDO LAND	ACTION	2012	4.21
4	SUPER SMASH BROS. FOR WII U AND 3DS	FIGHTING	2014	3.81
5	SUPER MARIO 3D WORLD	PLATFORM	2013	3.66
6	SPLATOON	SHOOTER	2015	2.25
7	NEW SUPER LUIGI U	PLATFORM	2013	2.14
8	WII PARTY U	PARTY	2013	1.65
9	THE LEGEND OF ZELDA: THE WIND WAKER	ACTION	2013	1.46
10	SUPER MARIO MAKER	PLATFORM	2015	1.39

TOP 10

BIGGEST WII GAMES

Although new Nintendo Wiis haven't been produced since 2013, gaming on it is still very popular...

Wii Fit was first released in Japan on
DEC 1, 2007

	NAME	GENRE	RELEASED	UNIT SALES (MILLIONS)
1	WII SPORTS	SPORTS	2006	82.57
2	MARIO KART WII	RACING	2008	35.4
3	WII SPORTS RESORT	SPORTS	2009	32.78
4	WII PLAY	PARTY	2006	28.94
5	NEW SUPER MARIO BROS. WII	PLATFORM	2009	28.2
6	WII FIT	SPORTS	2007	22.69
7	WII FIT PLUS	SPORTS	2009	21.84
8	SUPER SMASH BROS. BRAWL	FIGHTING	2008	12.75
9	SUPER MARIO GALAXY	PLATFORM	2007	11.34
10	JUST DANCE 3	PARTY	2011	10.13

GENRE FACE-OFF

Ranking the Wii's biggest hits by their style...

- SPORTS **4**
- PARTY **2**
- PLATFORM **2**
- RACING **1**
- FIGHTING **1**

JUST DANCE 3

10 The third game in this series was released on October 7, 2011. The *Just Dance* game franchise has shifted 57.3 million copies since the first game appeared in 2009.

WII FIT

6 The *Wii Fit* Balance Board can be used to play the slalom skiing and snowboard elements of the game. The activities can help strengthen core muscles.

BIGGEST-SELLING PS4 GAMES

TOP 10

This next-generation console is a clear hit for those who love action and shooting games...

	NAME	GENRE	RELEASED	UNIT SALES (MILLIONS)
1	GRAND THEFT AUTO V	ACTION	2014	8.21
2	CALL OF DUTY: ADVANCED WARFARE	SHOOTER	2014	7.08
3	FIFA 15	SPORTS	2014	6.47
4	CALL OF DUTY: BLACK OPS 3	SHOOTER	2015	5.55
5	DESTINY	ACTION	2014	5.24
6	FIFA 16	SPORTS	2015	5
7	WATCH DOGS	ACTION	2014	3.9
8	ASSASSIN'S CREED: UNITY	ACTION	2014	3.56
9	FAR CRY 4	SHOOTER	2014	3.55
10	THE LAST OF US	ADVENTURE	2014	3.54

CALL OF DUTY: ADVANCED WARFARE

2 Incorporating a sci-fi element, this *Call of Duty* title is set in the 2050s. American actor Kevin Spacey provides the voice for key character Jonathan Irons.

The first *Far Cry* game was released in **2004**

THE LAST OF US

10 First released on the PS3 on June 14, 2013, the remastered PS4 edition emerged the following year on July 29, 2014. The game has won over 120 international awards.

GRAND THEFT AUTO V

1

At the 2014 British Academy Games Awards, *Grand Theft Auto V* won three of its nine nominations, including Best Games Design.

The *Call of Duty* franchise has sold

230.84

MILLION

units

TOP 10

BIGGEST-SELLING PS3, PS2, & PLAYSTATION GAMES

Combining all three of Sony's previous home consoles, these were their best-selling titles...

	NAME	PLATFORM	GENRE	RELEASED	UNIT SALES (MILLIONS)
1	GRAND THEFT AUTO V	PS3	ACTION	2013	21.04
2	GRAND THEFT AUTO: SAN ANDREAS	PS2	ACTION	2004	20.81
3	GRAND THEFT AUTO: VICE CITY	PS2	ACTION	2002	16.15
4	GRAN TURISMO 3: A-SPEC	PS2	RACING	2001	14.98
5	CALL OF DUTY: BLACK OPS II	PS3	SHOOTER	2012	13.75
6	CALL OF DUTY: MODERN WARFARE 3	PS3	SHOOTER	2011	13.32
7	GRAND THEFT AUTO III	PS2	ACTION	2001	13.1
8	CALL OF DUTY: BLACK OPS	PS3	SHOOTER	2010	12.58
9	GRAN TURISMO 4	PS2	RACING	2004	11.66
10	GRAN TURISMO	PS	RACING	1997	10.95

GRAN TURISMO 4

9

This racing franchise has sold more than 71 million copies worldwide. *Gran Turismo 4* was released in Japan first on December 28, 2004.

TOP 10

BEST-SELLING PS VITA

Fans of action gaming on the go are still enjoying this six-year-old handheld gaming system...

Number of main *Persona* games in the *Shin Megami Tensei* franchise:

6

	NAME	GENRE	RELEASED	UNIT SALES (MILLIONS)
1	UNCHARTED: GOLDEN ABYSS	ACTION	2011	1.53
2	CALL OF DUTY: BLACK OPS: DECLASSIFIED	ACTION	2012	1.34
3	ASSASSIN'S CREED III: LIBERATION	ACTION	2012	1.32
4	LITTLEBIGPLANET PS VITA	PLATFORM	2012	1.2
=	MINECRAFT	ADVENTURE	2014	1.2
6	PERSONA 4: THE GOLDEN	RPG	2012	1.07
7	NEED FOR SPEED: MOST WANTED	RACING	2012	0.97
8	KILLZONE: MERCENARY	SHOOTER	2013	0.81
=	FINAL FANTASY X/X-2 HD REMASTER	RPG	2013	0.81
10	TEARAWAY	ACTION	2013	0.63

LITTLEBIGPLANET PS VITA

4 Since the 2008 LittleBigPlanet arrived on the PS3, this franchise has sold more than 16 million copies. The PS Vita's touchscreen allows for more ways to create levels.

DIFFERENT WAYS TO GAME

Here's how the PS Vita's biggest games compare by genre....

ACTION
4

RPG
2

PLATFORM
1

ADVENTURE
1

RACING
1

SHOOTER
1

NEED FOR SPEED: MOST WANTED

7 The nineteenth game in the *Need For Speed* franchise gave players the ability to compete in races of their choosing in an open world environment.

Number of *God of War* releases:
12

CRISIS CORE: FINAL FANTASY VII

10 Highly acclaimed Japanese composer Takeharu Ishimoto has written the music for several major games, including *Crisis Core: Final Fantasy VII* and *Dissidia Final Fantasy*, released November 26, 2015.

DAXTER

5 This game spun out of the *Jak and Daxter* series, which began in 2001 with *Jak and Daxter: The Precursor Legacy* for the PS2. Daxter (the sixth release) is set between that debut game and 2003's *Jak II*.

TOP 10

BEST-SELLING PSP

It lasted 10 years as a handheld console, and these were the games that counted the most...

	NAME	GENRE	RELEASED	UNIT SALES (MILLIONS)
1	GRAND THEFT AUTO: LIBERTY CITY STORIES	ACTION	2005	**7.68**
2	MONSTER HUNTER FREEDOM UNITE	RPG	2008	**5.48**
3	GRAND THEFT AUTO: VICE CITY STORIES	ACTION	2006	**5.04**
4	MONSTER HUNTER FREEDOM 3	RPG	2010	**4.87**
▶**5**	DAXTER	PLATFORM	2006	**4.17**
6	RATCHET & CLANK: SIZE MATTERS	PLATFORM	2007	**3.74**
7	MIDNIGHT CLUB 3: DUB EDITION	RACING	2005	**3.64**
8	GRAN TURISMO	RACING	2009	**3.24**
9	GOD OF WAR: CHAINS OF OLYMPUS	ACTION	2008	**3.17**
▶**10**	CRISIS CORE: FINAL FANTASY VII	RPG	2007	**3.16**

Titanfall was released on

3

platforms

DESTINY

5 This first-person shooter was developed by Bungie, the team behind the *Halo* franchise. Its original soundtrack included new music by Paul McCartney.

FORZA MOTORSPORT 5

10 Exclusive to the Xbox One console, this racing game has 200 cars to choose from, with more available as downloadable content. Players can race on more than 20 circuits.

TOP 10

BIGGEST-SELLING XBOX ONE GAMES

Microsoft's latest home console, like its 360 predecessor, is beloved by shooting game fans...

	NAME	GENRE	RELEASED	UNIT SALES (MILLIONS)
1	CALL OF DUTY: ADVANCED WARFARE	SHOOTER	2014	4.73
2	GRAND THEFT AUTO V	ACTION	2014	3.37
3	CALL OF DUTY: BLACK OPS 3	SHOOTER	2015	3.31
4	ASSASSIN'S CREED: UNITY	ACTION	2014	3.06
5	DESTINY	ACTION	2014	3.01
6	TITANFALL	SHOOTER	2014	2.71
7	HALO: THE MASTER CHIEF COLLECTION	SHOOTER	2014	2.67
8	CALL OF DUTY: GHOSTS	SHOOTER	2013	2.62
9	ASSASSIN'S CREED IV: BLACK FLAG	ACTION	2013	2.11
10	FORZA MOTORSPORT 5	RACING	2013	2.05

TOP 10

BIGGEST-SELLING XBOX 360 GAMES

The *Call of Duty* franchise sold millions on this system, but the number one belongs to a party game...

	NAME	GENRE	RELEASED	UNIT SALES (MILLIONS)
1	KINECT ADVENTURES!	PARTY	2010	21.63
2	GRAND THEFT AUTO V	ACTION	2013	15.6
3	CALL OF DUTY: MODERN WARFARE 3	SHOOTER	2011	14.59
4	CALL OF DUTY: BLACK OPS	SHOOTER	2010	14.41
5	CALL OF DUTY: BLACK OPS II	SHOOTER	2012	13.49
6	CALL OF DUTY: MODERN WARFARE 2	SHOOTER	2009	13.44
7	HALO 3	SHOOTER	2007	12.06
8	GRAND THEFT AUTO IV	ACTION	2008	10.94
9	CALL OF DUTY: GHOSTS	SHOOTER	2013	9.87
10	HALO: REACH	SHOOTER	2010	9.77

HALO 2

Released on the Xbox console, *Halo 2* (2004) almost rivalled the sales in this top 10 with worldwide unit sales of 8.49 million.

The first *Grand Theft Auto* game was released in

1997

KINECT ADVENTURES!

1 Released on November 4, 2010, this launch title for the Xbox 360's Kinect motion-camera system has not spawned any sequels. Its five challenge areas require full-body movement/ interaction with the puzzles on-screen.

DEVIL MAY CRY 4 (ACTION)

1 Capcom's *Devil May Cry* action series has sold 15.1 million units. *Devil May Cry 4: Special Edition* was released on PS4 and Xbox One on June 18, 2015.

Total sales of the adventure genre:

237.81 MILLION

DEAD SPACE 3 (SHOOTER)

3 Developer Visceral Games' *Dead Space* saga includes six games and several tie-in comics, novels, and animated films. *Dead Space 3* was largely set on ice-planet Tau Volantis.

MOST SUCCESSFUL GENRES

TOP 10

Combining games of all types, across all platforms, here are the genres that sell the most units...

	GENRE	ALL PLATFORMS' UNIT SALES (MILLIONS)
1	ACTION	1,648.08
2	SPORTS	1,279.45
3	SHOOTER	958.86
4	RPG	881.35
5	PLATFORM	815.05
6	PARTY	782.19
7	RACING	716.08
8	FIGHTING	435.94
9	SIMULATION	382.3
10	PUZZLE	242.63

GENRE WINNERS

Here's how the top 5 compare visually...

ACTION 1,648.08 MILLION

SPORTS 1,279.45 MILLION

SHOOTER 958.86 MILLION

RPG 881.35 MILLION

PLATFORM 815.05 MILLION

TOP 10

GENRE BEST-SELLERS

Taking a look at each genre, here are the biggest sellers from each of those kinds of games...

	GENRE	GAME	RELEASED	PLATFORM	UNIT SALES (MILLIONS)
1	SPORTS	WII SPORTS	2006	WII	82.57
2	PLATFORM	SUPER MARIO BROS.	1985	NES	40.24
3	RACING	MARIO KART WII	2008	WII	35.4
4	RPG	POKÉMON RED/BLUE/GREEN	1996	GAME BOY	31.37
5	PUZZLE	TETRIS	1989	GAME BOY	30.26
6	PARTY	WII PLAY	2006	WII	28.94
7	SHOOTER	DUCK HUNT	1984	NES	28.31
8	SIMULATION	NINTENDOGS	2005	DS	24.69
9	ACTION	GRAND THEFT AUTO: SAN ANDREAS	2004	PS2	20.81
10	FIGHTING	SUPER SMASH BROS. BRAWL	2008	WII	12.75

Tetris has appeared in

71

games

GRAND THEFT AUTO: SAN ANDREAS

9 Released across multiple platforms between 2004 and 2015, the *San Andreas* sub-brand of *Grand Theft Auto* has itself sold nearly 24 million units.

SUPER MARIO BROS.

2 Japanese composer Koji Kondo wrote the iconic music for not only *Super Mario Bros.* and *Super Mario Bros. 2* (pictured), but also numerous other Nintendo games. He has worked for Nintendo since 1984.

111

Final Fantasy games have shifted more than **110 MILLION** units

LEGO

7 Across all gaming platforms, there have been 230 official LEGO video games made since 1997. *LEGO Marvel's Avengers* was released on January 26, 2016.

SONIC THE HEDGEHOG

8 The super-fast blue hero debuted on the Sega Megadrive in 1991 in *Sonic The Hedgehog*. The latest title, *Sonic Boom: Fire & Ice*, was released in 2016 for Nintendo 3DS.

TOP 10

BIGGEST GAME BRANDS

Come up with a popular character or series, and your unit sales could go into the hundreds of millions...

	FRANCHISE	UNIT SALES (MILLIONS)
1	SUPER MARIO BROS.	580.83
2	POKÉMON	244.98
3	CALL OF DUTY	230.66
4	WII FIT/SPORTS/PARTY	199.8
5	GRAND THEFT AUTO	159.54
6	FIFA	158.02
▶ 7	LEGO	126.25
▷ 8	SONIC THE HEDGEHOG	114.24
9	FINAL FANTASY	110.03
10	NEED FOR SPEED	98.33

BATMAN: ARKHAM CITY

1 There have been four game in the *Batman: Arkham* series released between 2009 and 2015. Across all platforms, the second game of the franchise, *Batman: Arkham City,* has sold 11.03 million units.

Across all platforms, *LEGO Batman: The Videogame* has sold

13.3 MILLION units

SPIDER-MAN: THE MOVIE

3 Based on the 2002 movie directed by Sam Raimi, this Spider-Man game includes narration by Bruce Campbell. The *Ash vs. Evil Dead* star cameoed as the ring announcer in the film.

TOP 10

BIGGEST SUPERHERO GAMES

Those caped crusaders don't just sell millions of movie theatre tickets, they triumph in the gaming market too...

	NAME	PLATFORM	RELEASED	UNIT SALES (MILLIONS)
1	BATMAN: ARKHAM CITY	PS3	2011	5.37
2	BATMAN: ARKHAM CITY	XBOX 360	2011	4.67
3	SPIDER-MAN: THE MOVIE	PS2	2002	4.48
4	BATMAN: ARKHAM ASYLUM	PS3	2009	4.19
5	BATMAN: ARKHAM ASYLUM	XBOX 360	2009	3.44
6	SPIDER-MAN 2	PS2	2004	3.41
7	BATMAN: ARKHAM KNIGHT	PS4	2015	3.37
8	LEGO BATMAN: THE VIDEOGAME	XBOX 360	2008	3.33
9	SPIDER-MAN	PS	2000	3.13
10	LEGO BATMAN: THE VIDEOGAME	WII	2008	3.06

BIGGEST TOLKIEN TIE-IN GAMES

The expansive world of Middle Earth has inspired dozens of very different video games since 1982...

	NAME	PLATFORM	RELEASED	UNIT SALES (MILLIONS)
1	THE LORD OF THE RINGS: THE TWO TOWERS	PS2	2002	**4.67**
2	THE LORD OF THE RINGS: THE RETURN OF THE KING	PS2	2003	**3.28**
3	MIDDLE-EARTH: SHADOW OF MORDOR	PS4	2014	**2.52**
4	LEGO THE LORD OF THE RINGS	XBOX 360	2012	**1.21**
5	THE LORD OF THE RINGS: THE FELLOWSHIP OF THE RING	PS2	2002	**1.2**
6	THE LORD OF THE RINGS: THE RETURN OF THE KING	XBOX	2003	**1.14**
7	MIDDLE-EARTH: SHADOW OF MORDOR	XBOX ONE	2014	**1.1**
8	LEGO THE LORD OF THE RINGS	PS3	2012	**1.06**
9	LEGO THE LORD OF THE RINGS	WII	2012	**0.91**
10	THE LORD OF THE RINGS: WAR IN THE NORTH	PS3	2011	**0.84**

THE LORD OF THE RINGS: THE RETURN OF THE KING

6 This tie-in game saw Elijah Wood reprise his role as Frodo Baggins. His voice performance won a 2004 DICE (Design, Innovate, Communicate, Entertain) award.

MIDDLE-EARTH: SHADOW OF MORDOR

3 Set during the 60-year period between the storylines of *The Hobbit* and *The Lord of the Rings*, this was developed by Monolith Productions.

J. R. R. Tolkien wrote *The Lord of the Rings* over a period of

12 years

125

TOP 10

BIGGEST ZELDA GAMES

Ever since Link appeared in the 1986 debut title, the Zelda franchise has garnered millions of fans worldwide...

	NAME	PLATFORM	RELEASED	UNIT SALES (MILLIONS)
1	THE LEGEND OF ZELDA: OCARINA OF TIME	N64	1998	7.6
▶ 2	THE LEGEND OF ZELDA: TWILIGHT PRINCESS	WII	2006	7.18
3	THE LEGEND OF ZELDA	NES	1986	6.51
4	THE LEGEND OF ZELDA: THE PHANTOM HOURGLASS	DS	2007	5.1
5	THE LEGEND OF ZELDA: A LINK TO THE PAST	SNES	1991	4.61
6	THE LEGEND OF ZELDA: THE WIND WAKER	GAMECUBE	2002	4.6
7	ZELDA II: THE ADVENTURE OF LINK	NES	1987	4.38
▷ 8	THE LEGEND OF ZELDA: SKYWARD SWORD	WII	2011	3.98
9	THE LEGEND OF ZELDA: LINK'S AWAKENING	GAME BOY	1992	3.83
10	THE LEGEND OF ZELDA: OCARINA OF TIME	3DS	2011	3.82

THE LEGEND OF ZELDA: SKYWARD SWORD

8 Although it is the sixteenth title in the series, this prequel is set before any other *Zelda* game. It was released on November 18, 2011 exclusively for the Nintendo Wii.

THE LEGEND OF ZELDA: TWILIGHT PRINCESS

2 The thirteenth *Zelda* game was originally planned for release on the GameCube, Nintendo's predecessor to the Wii. In 2016, an HD version was released for the Wii U.

The Legend Of Zelda: Tri-Force Heroes was released on **OCT 22, 2015**

STAR WARS: BATTLEFRONT

9 On November 17, 2015, eleven years after the hit PS2 version, a brand new take on this *Star Wars* game franchise was released for the PS4 and Xbox One.

THE SIMPSONS: ROAD RAGE

9 This is the nineteenth official video game based on *The Simpsons*. Since 1991, there have been 25 games based on the Matt Groening-created TV show.

Across all platforms, the *LEGO Indiana Jones* games have sold
16.98
MILLION
units

BIGGEST MOVIE/TV TIE-IN GAMES

TOP 10

There have been hundreds of official video games made of TV/film franchises, including these 10 best-sellers...

	NAME	GENRE	PLATFORM	RELEASED	UNIT SALES (MILLIONS)
1	GOLDENEYE 007	SHOOTER	N64	1997	8.09
2	LEGO STAR WARS: THE COMPLETE SAGA	ACTION	WII	2007	5.61
3	LEGO STAR WARS: THE COMPLETE SAGA	ACTION	DS	2007	4.76
4	THE SIMPSONS: HIT & RUN	RACING	PS2	2003	4.7
5	THE LORD OF THE RINGS: THE TWO TOWERS	ACTION	PS2	2002	4.67
6	SPIDER-MAN: THE MOVIE	ACTION	PS2	2002	4.48
7	LEGO INDIANA JONES: THE ORIGINAL ADVENTURES	ADVENTURE	XBOX 360	2008	3.74
8	HARRY POTTER & THE SORCERER'S STONE	ACTION	PS	2001	3.73
9	STAR WARS: BATTLEFRONT	SHOOTER	PS2	2004	3.61
=	THE SIMPSONS: ROAD RAGE	RACING	PS2	2001	3.61

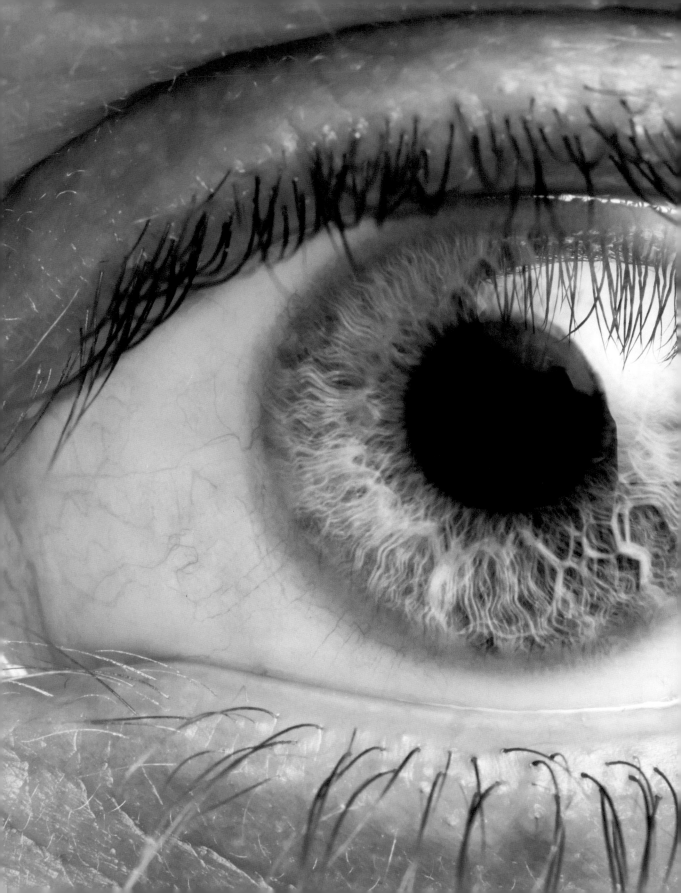

HUMANKIND

ZONE **5**

MOST POPULATED COUNTRIES

TOP 10

Of all the 196 recognized countries on Earth, these are inhabited by the most humans...

	COUNTRY	POPULATION
1	CHINA	1,373,180,000
2	INDIA	1,280,040,000
3	USA	322,230,000
4	INDONESIA	255,461,700
5	BRAZIL	205,190,000
6	PAKISTAN	188,925,000
7	NIGERIA	182,202,000
8	BANGLADESH	159,365,000
9	RUSSIA	146,435,680
10	JAPAN	126,890,000

CHINA

1 This country's official full name is the People's Republic of China. The population of its capital city, Beijing (measured by its core districts) is 11.72 million.

USA

3 The United States of America's Declaration of Independence (from the British Empire) was approved and issued in Philadelphia, Pennsylvania on July 4, 1776.

California is the most populated state in the USA:

38.8 MILLION

Liechtenstein's size:

61 MI²

VATICAN CITY

1 Located inside a series of walls in Rome, Italy, Vatican City has been recognized as a country since February 11, 1929.

NAURU

3 An island in the central region of the Pacific Ocean, Nauru is just over 8 mi² (20.9 km²). Its capital, Yaren, is home to an underground lake called the Moqua Well.

TOP 10

LEAST POPULATED COUNTRIES

This top 10 contains countries that have a smaller population than most large towns in the UK...

	COUNTRY	POPULATION
1	VATICAN CITY	839
2	NIUE	1,490
3	NAURU	10,084
4	TUVALU	10,640
5	COOK ISLANDS	14,974
6	PALAU	20,901
7	SAN MARINO	32,831
8	LIECHTENSTEIN	37,370
9	MONACO	37,800
10	SOUTH OSSETIA	51,547

SMALLEST POPULATIONS

Here is how the top 5 compare graphically...

COOK ISLANDS
14,974

NAURU
10,084

TUVALU
10,640

VATICAN CITY
839

NIUE
1,490

131

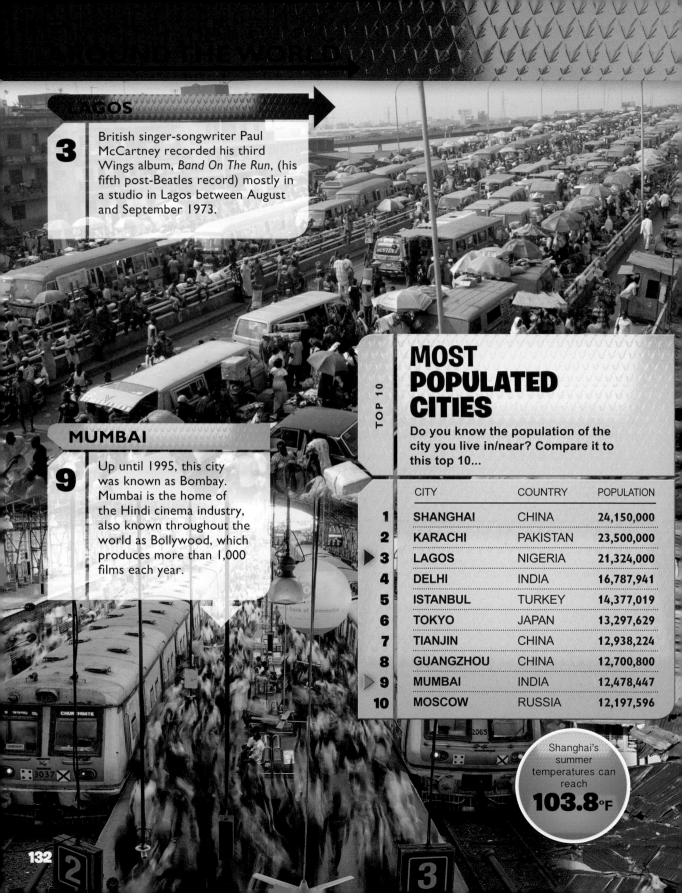

LAGOS

3 British singer-songwriter Paul McCartney recorded his third Wings album, *Band On The Run*, (his fifth post-Beatles record) mostly in a studio in Lagos between August and September 1973.

MUMBAI

9 Up until 1995, this city was known as Bombay. Mumbai is the home of the Hindi cinema industry, also known throughout the world as Bollywood, which produces more than 1,000 films each year.

TOP 10

MOST POPULATED CITIES

Do you know the population of the city you live in/near? Compare it to this top 10...

	CITY	COUNTRY	POPULATION
1	SHANGHAI	CHINA	24,150,000
2	KARACHI	PAKISTAN	23,500,000
3	LAGOS	NIGERIA	21,324,000
4	DELHI	INDIA	16,787,941
5	ISTANBUL	TURKEY	14,377,019
6	TOKYO	JAPAN	13,297,629
7	TIANJIN	CHINA	12,938,224
8	GUANGZHOU	CHINA	12,700,800
9	MUMBAI	INDIA	12,478,447
10	MOSCOW	RUSSIA	12,197,596

Shanghai's summer temperatures can reach **103.8°F**

MADRID

10 The Manzanares river flows through the Spanish capital. Popular with fishing enthusiasts, species such as carp, pike, and common and rainbow trout can be found in the river.

Wenzhou's first ever railway opened **JUN 11, 1998**

NAIROBI

7 Kenya's largest city (which is also its capital) is home to the country's oldest hospital. Established in 1901, the Kenyatta National Hospital has a staff of over 6,000.

TOP 10

LEAST POPULATED CITIES

Of all the places officially classified as a city, these have the lowest population figures...

	CITY	COUNTRY	POPULATION
1	**WENZHOU**	CHINA	3,039,439
2	**BUENOS AIRES**	ARGENTINA	3,054,300
3	**JAIPUR**	INDIA	3,073,350
4	**ADDIS ABABA**	ETHIOPIA	3,103,673
5	**PUNE**	INDIA	3,115,431
6	**ZHONGSHAN**	CHINA	3,121,275
7	**NAIROBI**	KENYA	3,138,369
8	**EKURHULENI**	SOUTH AFRICA	3,178,470
9	**PESHAWAR**	PAKISTAN	3,201,000
10	**MADRID**	SPAIN	3,207,247

SELMA LAGERLÖF

10 Born on November 20, 1858, Lagerlöf was the first woman to be awarded the Nobel Prize in Literature. Her other honours include becoming the first woman to be featured on Swedish currency (her face adorns the 20 Kronor bill).

RUDYARD KIPLING

8 Known for such works as *The Jungle Book* (1894) and *Just So Stories* (1902), the British writer was born in 1865 in the then British-ruled part of India, Bombay (now called Mumbai).

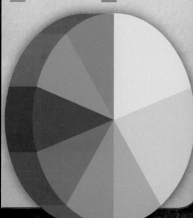

Bjørnstjerne Bjørnson total published works:

32

TOP 10

FIRST NOBEL PRIZE IN LITERATURE WINNERS

This coveted prize celebrates outstanding contributions in the artistic area of literature...

	NAME	COUNTRY	YEAR
1	SULLY PRUDHOMME	FRANCE	1901
2	THEODOR MOMMSEN	GERMANY	1902
3	BJØRNSTJERNE BJØRNSON	NORWAY	1903
4	FRÉDÉRIC MISTRAL	FRANCE	1904
=	JOSÉ ECHEGARAY	SPAIN	1904
6	HENRYK SIENKIEWICZ	POLAND	1905
7	GIOSUÈ CARDUCCI	ITALY	1906
8	RUDYARD KIPLING	UK	1907
9	RUDOLF CHRISTOPH EUCKEN	GERMANY	1908
10	SELMA LAGERLÖF	SWEDEN	1909

WINNING NATIONS

Ranked by country, this top 10 is almost an even split...

FRANCE
GERMANY
NORWAY
SPAIN

POLAND
ITALY
UK
SWEDEN

SAUL PERLMUTTER

This American astrophysicist also won the 2015 Fundamental Physics Prize for his part in discovering the expansion of the universe accelerating, not slowing down.

ARTHUR B. MCDONALD

1 Aged 73, McDonald is a board member of the Perimeter Institute for Theoretical Physics, based in his home province of Ontario, Canada.

MOST RECENT NOBEL PRIZE IN PHYSICS WINNERS

TOP 10

Winners are awarded for their highly significant scientific work in the physics spectrum...

	NAME	COUNTRY	YEAR
1	ARTHUR B. MCDONALD	CANADA	2015
=	TAKAAKI KAJITA	JAPAN	2015
3	SHUJI NAKAMURA	JAPAN	2014
=	HIROSHI AMANO	JAPAN	2014
=	ISAMU AKASAKI	JAPAN	2014
6	PETER HIGGS	UK	2013
=	FRANÇOIS ENGLERT	BELGIUM	2013
8	DAVID J. WINELAND	USA	2012
=	SERGE HAROCHE	FRANCE	2012
10	SAUL PERLMUTTER, ADAM G. RIESS & BRIAN P. SCHMIDT	USA & AUSTRALIA	2011

David J. Wineland was born **FEB 24, 1944**

LONGEST REIGNING MONARCHS OF ALL TIME

All of these entries in this top 10 remained on their respective thrones for more than seven decades...

	NAME	LOCATION	REIGN BEGAN	REIGN ENDED	TOTAL TIME
1	SOBHUZA II	SWAZILAND	DEC 10, 1899	AUG 21, 1982	82 YEARS, 254 DAYS
2	BERNHARD VII	LIPPE (HOLY ROMAN EMPIRE)	AUG 12, 1429	APR 2, 1511	81 YEARS, 234 DAYS
3	WILLIAM IV	HENNEBERG-SCHLEUSINGEN (HOLY ROMAN EMPIRE)	MAY 26, 1480	JAN 24, 1559	78 YEARS, 243 DAYS
4	HEINRICH XI	REUSS-OBERGREIZ (HOLY ROMAN EMPIRE)	MAR 17, 1723	JUN 28, 1800	77 YEARS, 103 DAYS
5	IDRIS IBNI MUHAMMAD AL-QADRI	TAMPIN (MALAYSIA)	MAY 1, 1929	DEC 26, 2005	76 YEARS, 239 DAYS
6	CHRISTIAN AUGUST	PALATINATE-SULZBACH (HOLY ROMAN EMPIRE)	AUG 14, 1632	APR 23, 1708	75 YEARS, 253 DAYS
7	MUDHOJI IV RAO NAIK NIMBALKAR	PHALTAN STATE (INDIA)	DEC 7, 1841	OCT 17, 1916	74 YEARS, 315 DAYS
8	BHAGVATSINGH SAHIB	GONDAL STATE (INDIA)	DEC 14, 1869	MAR 10, 1944	74 YEARS, 87 DAYS
9	GEORG WILHELM	SCHAUMBURG-LIPPE (HOLY ROMAN EMPIRE)	FEB 13, 1787	NOV 21, 1860	73 YEARS, 282 DAYS
10	KARL FRIEDRICH	BADEN (HOLY ROMAN EMPIRE)	MAY 12, 1738	JUN 10, 1811	73 YEARS, 29 DAYS

Sobhuza II was born on **JUL 22, 1899**

LIPPE FAMILY

The House of Lippe (coat of arms shown) presided over Germany's principality of Lippe from 1123 to 1918.

BHAGVATSINGH SAHIB

8 Born October 24, 1865 in Dhoraji, Gujarat, India, Sahib received numerous political and academic honours throughout his life. These included a Bachelor of Medicine.

EPIC
STRUCTURES

ZONE **6**

LARGEST ALL-RESIDENTIAL BUILDINGS

Some skyscrapers combine offices and homes, but these are just for residents...

	BUILDING	CITY	COUNTRY	YEAR COMPLETED	FLOORS	HEIGHT (M)	(FT)
1	PRINCESS TOWER	DUBAI	UNITED ARAB EMIRATES	2012	101	413.4	1,356
2	23 MARINA	DUBAI	UNITED ARAB EMIRATES	2012	88	392.4	1,287
3	BURJ MOHAMMED BIN RASHID TOWER	ABU DHABI	UNITED ARAB EMIRATES	2014	88	381.2	1,251
4	ELITE RESIDENCE	DUBAI	UNITED ARAB EMIRATES	2012	87	380.5	1,248
5	THE TORCH	DUBAI	UNITED ARAB EMIRATES	2011	86	352	1,155
6	Q1 TOWER	GOLD COAST	AUSTRALIA	2005	78	322.5	1,058
7	HHHR TOWER	DUBAI	UNITED ARAB EMIRATES	2010	72	317.6	1,042
8	OCEAN HEIGHTS	DUBAI	UNITED ARAB EMIRATES	2010	83	310	1,017
9	CAYAN TOWER	DUBAI	UNITED ARAB EMIRATES	2013	73	306.4	1,005
10	EAST PACIFIC CENTER TOWER A	SHENZHEN	CHINA	2013	85	306	1,004

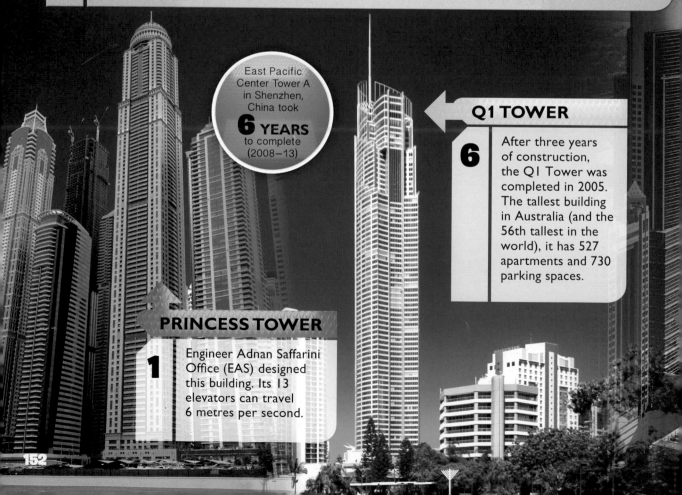

East Pacific Center Tower A in Shenzhen, China took **6** YEARS to complete (2008–13)

Q1 TOWER

6 After three years of construction, the Q1 Tower was completed in 2005. The tallest building in Australia (and the 56th tallest in the world), it has 527 apartments and 730 parking spaces.

PRINCESS TOWER

1 Engineer Adnan Saffarini Office (EAS) designed this building. Its 13 elevators can travel 6 metres per second.

SCRAPING THE SKY

These cities have the most giant buildings...

NYC
1,204

HONG KONG
550

CHICAGO
413

TORONTO
384

SHANGHAI
269

Number of Shanghai buildings taller than 492 ft (150 m):

126

TOP 10

CITIES WITH THE MOST SKYSCRAPERS

If you walk the streets of these places, you'll spend most of your time staring upwards...

	CITY	COUNTRY	TOTAL SKYSCRAPERS
1	NEW YORK CITY	USA	1,204
2	HONG KONG	CHINA	550
▶ 3	CHICAGO	USA	413
4	TORONTO	CANADA	384
5	SHANGHAI	CHINA	269
▷ 6	DUBAI	UNITED ARAB EMIRATES	253
7	SYDNEY	AUSTRALIA	194
8	TOKYO	JAPAN	189
9	HOUSTON	USA	175
10	MELBOURNE	AUSTRALIA	163

DUBAI

6 With an average building age of seven years, Dubai's population of over 2.2 million inhabits a very modern-looking city. Proposed in 2015, the 2,333-ft (711-m) tall Dubai One will be complete by 2020.

CHICAGO

3 Over 60 per cent of Chicago's buildings are made primarily of concrete. Over 47 per cent of the city's constructions are used for offices.

BIGGEST BUILDS

China's Shanghai World Financial Center has **91** elevators

RUSSIA

4 Along with its four completed 300 m+ buildings, Russia's capital city Moscow has a further two under development. The 1,226-ft (373.7-m) high Federation Towers opened in 2016.

COUNTRIES WITH THE MOST 300 M+ BUILDINGS

These are the nations that have constructed the giant towers that dwarf all others...

USA

3 Started in 2014 and planned for a 2019 opening, New York City's Central Park Tower will be 1,775 ft (541 m) high. It will contain residential, retail, and hotel facilities.

	COUNTRY	NUMBER OF 300 M+ BUILDINGS
1	CHINA	36
2	UNITED ARAB EMIRATES	22
3	USA	16
4	RUSSIA	4
5	MALAYSIA	3
=	SAUDI ARABIA	3
7	SOUTH KOREA	2
=	TAIWAN	2
=	KUWAIT	2
10	AUSTRALIA/CHILE/JAPAN/QATAR/THAILAND/UK/VIETNAM	1

Bibliothèque Nationale de France was first opened to the public in
1692

NATIONAL LIBRARY OF CHINA

9 Established in 1909, this was originally called the Imperial Library of Peking. Among its vast collection are over 1.6 million ancient handmade Chinese texts.

TOP 10

BIGGEST LIBRARIES

Does your local library have your favourite books? Next time you visit, find out if their inventory rivals these...

	NAME	CITY	COUNTRY	NUMBER OF BOOKS
1	THE BRITISH LIBRARY	LONDON	UK	170 MILLION
2	LIBRARY OF CONGRESS	WASHINGTON D.C.	USA	160 MILLION
3	LIBRARY AND ARCHIVES	OTTAWA	CANADA	54 MILLION
4	NEW YORK PUBLIC LIBRARY	NEW YORK CITY	USA	53.1 MILLION
5	RUSSIAN STATE LIBRARY	MOSCOW	RUSSIA	44.4 MILLION
6	BIBLIOTHÈQUE NATIONALE DE FRANCE	PARIS	FRANCE	40 MILLION
7	NATIONAL LIBRARY OF RUSSIA	ST PETERSBURG	RUSSIA	36.5 MILLION
8	NATIONAL DIET LIBRARY	TOKYO/KYOTO	JAPAN	35.6 MILLION
9	NATIONAL LIBRARY OF CHINA	BEIJING	CHINA	31.2 MILLION
10	ROYAL DANISH LIBRARY	COPENHAGEN	DENMARK	30.2 MILLION

LIBRARY OF CONGRESS

2 Thomas Jefferson's own collection of 6,487 books was bought by Congress for this library in 1815. There are also books featuring 460 different languages.

155

SHANGHAI WORLD FINANCIAL CENTER

Jin Mao Tower's total parking spaces: **993**

3 11 years in the making, this, the second tallest building in China, was opened in 2008. The two arcs and square prism echo the Chinese symbols for heaven and earth.

TOP 10

BIGGEST HOTELS

If you enjoy a room with a view, these are the 10 hotels you need to put on your holiday wish list...

	BUILDING	COUNTRY	YEAR COMPLETED	FLOORS	ROOMS	HEIGHT (M)	(FT)
1	BURJ KHALIFA	UNITED ARAB EMIRATES	2010	163	304	828	2,717
2	MAKKAH ROYAL CLOCK TOWER HOTEL	SAUDI ARABIA	2012	120	858	601	1,972
3	SHANGHAI WORLD FINANCIAL CENTER	CHINA	2008	101	174	492	1,614
4	INTERNATIONAL COMMERCE CENTRE	CHINA	2010	108	312	484	1,588
5	ZIFENG TOWER	CHINA	2010	66	450	450	1,476
6	KK100	CHINA	2011	100	249	441.8	1,449
7	GUANGZHOU INTERNATIONAL FINANCE CENTER	CHINA	2010	103	374	438.6	1,439
8	TRUMP INTERNATIONAL HOTEL & TOWER	USA	2009	98	339	423.2	1,389
9	JIN MAO TOWER	CHINA	1999	88	555	420.5	1,380
10	JW MARRIOTT MARQUIS HOTEL DUBAI TOWERS	UNITED ARAB EMIRATES	2012 & 2013	82	1,608*	355.4	1,166

Split between the two towers.

BURJ KHALIFA

1 This tower has more than 2,000,000 sq ft (185,800 sq m) of specially designed interiors, ranging from celestial to elemental influences.

MOST FLOORS OF ALL

Ranked by floors, these are the top 5...

BURJ KHALIFA	MAKKAH ROYAL CLOCK TOWER HOTEL	INTERNATIONAL COMMERCE CENTER	GUANGZHOU INTERNATIONAL FINANCE CENTER	SHANGHAI WORLD FINANCIAL CENTER
163	120	108	103	101

Tokyo Haneda Airport's early incarnation as Haneda Airfield opened in

1931

LONDON HEATHROW AIRPORT

3 Since its airfield beginnings in 1929, Heathrow now serves nearly 100 airlines that take passengers to 170 countries. Its fifth terminal, to cope with increased usage, was opened March 27, 2008.

BEIJING CAPITAL INTERNATIONAL AIRPORT

2 The first incarnation of this airport opened on March 2, 1958. In 2009 it was awarded the World's Best Airport by a renowned travel magazine.

TOP 10

AIRPORTS WITH THE MOST PASSENGERS

When it comes to air travel, these 10 complexes have the highest usage...

	AIRPORT	LOCATION	TOTAL PASSENGERS PER YEAR (MILLIONS)
1	HARTSFIELD–JACKSON ATLANTA INTERNATIONAL AIRPORT	GEORGIA (USA)	96.18
2	BEIJING CAPITAL INTERNATIONAL AIRPORT	BEIJING (CHINA)	86.13
3	LONDON HEATHROW AIRPORT	LONDON (UK)	73.41
4	TOKYO HANEDA AIRPORT	TOKYO (JAPAN)	72.83
5	LOS ANGELES INTERNATIONAL AIRPORT	CALIFORNIA (USA)	70.67
6	DUBAI INTERNATIONAL AIRPORT	DUBAI (UNITED ARAB EMIRATES)	70.48
7	O'HARE INTERNATIONAL AIRPORT	ILLINOIS (USA)	70.02
8	PARIS-CHARLES DE GAULLE AIRPORT	ÎLE-DE-FRANCE (FRANCE)	63.81
9	DALLAS-FORT WORTH INTERNATIONAL AIRPORT	TEXAS (USA)	63.52
10	HONG KONG INTERNATIONAL AIRPORT	HONG KONG (CHINA)	63.15

TALLEST CONSTRUCTIONS

PETRONAS TWIN TOWERS

7 These offices in Kuala Lumpur were begun in 1992. The connective structure is a skybridge between the 41st and 42nd floors. Facilities around these floors, such as a prayer room, can be shared.

TAIPEI 101

4 Being in a typhoon-prone region of the world, this building contains a 728-ton pendulum device that counters any movement caused by intense winds.

Construction of the Willis Tower took four years and was completed in
1974

TALLEST BUILDINGS

TOP 10

In the battle of the highest constructions in the world, these are the 10 victors...

	BUILDING	COUNTRY	YEAR COMPLETED	FLOORS	HEIGHT (M)	(FT)
1	BURJ KHALIFA	UNITED ARAB EMIRATES	2010	163	828	2,717
2	MAKKAH ROYAL CLOCK TOWER HOTEL	SAUDI ARABIA	2012	120	601	1,972
3	ONE WORLD TRADE CENTER	USA	2014	104	541	1,776
4	TAIPEI 101	TAIWAN	2004	101	508	1,667
5	SHANGHAI WORLD FINANCIAL CENTER	CHINA	2008	101	492	1,614
6	INTERNATIONAL COMMERCE CENTER	CHINA	2010	108	484	1,588
7	PETRONAS TWIN TOWERS	MALAYSIA	1998	88	451.9	1,483
8	ZIFENG TOWER	CHINA	2010	66	450	1,476
9	WILLIS TOWER	USA	1974	108	442.1	1,451
10	KK100	CHINA	2011	100	441.8	1,449

TOP 10

BUILDINGS WITH THE MOST FLOORS

Spires and other attributes aside, this chart is all about the number of floors above ground level...

	BUILDING	CITY	COUNTRY	YEAR COMPLETED	FLOORS
1	BURJ KHALIFA	DUBAI	UNITED ARAB EMIRATES	2010	**163**
2	MAKKAH ROYAL CLOCK TOWER HOTEL	MECCA	SAUDI ARABIA	2012	**120**
▷ 3	INTERNATIONAL COMMERCE CENTRE	HONG KONG	CHINA	2010	**108**
=	WILLIS TOWER	CHICAGO	USA	1974	**108**
5	GUANGZHOU INTERNATIONAL FINANCE CENTER	GUANGZHOU	CHINA	2010	**103**
▶ 6	EMPIRE STATE BUILDING	NEW YORK CITY	USA	1931	**102**
7	TAIPEI 101	TAIPEI	TAIWAN	2004	**101**
=	SHANGHAI WORLD FINANCIAL CENTER	SHANGHAI	CHINA	2008	**101**
=	PRINCESS TOWER	DUBAI	UNITED ARAB EMIRATES	2012	**101**
10	KK100/JOHN HANCOCK CENTER	SHENZHEN/CHICAGO	CHINA/USA	2011/1969	**100**

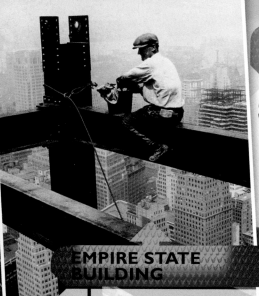

INTERNATIONAL COMMERCE CENTRE

3 83 elevators serve this building. An ample 1,700 parking spaces feature, with 312 hotel rooms as part of the complex. It also has four floors below ground level.

EMPIRE STATE BUILDING

6 Located at 350 5th Avenue, this building was completed in just one year, from 1930–31. It is the star of countless films including the 1933 and 2005 versions of *King Kong*.

John Hancock Center's global ranking for tallest building:

37TH

TALLEST CONSTRUCTIONS

Transamerica Pyramid is the tallest building in San Francisco, USA:

853 FT

LOS ANGELES

2 95 per cent of buildings in the City of Angels are made primarily from steel. Three towers of the Oceanwide Plaza are set to be completed by 2018.

SEOUL

1 Over 60 per cent of the buildings in South Korea's capital are residential. Along with the 70 buildings that exceed 492 ft (150 m) in height, there are currently a further ten under construction.

TOP 10

CITIES WITH THE MOST HELIPADS

Helicopter travel provides amazing views of any city, but these cities have the most places to land one...

	CITY	COUNTRY	NUMBER OF 200 M+ BUILDINGS WITH HELIPADS
1	SEOUL	SOUTH KOREA	12
2	BUSAN	SOUTH KOREA	10
=	LOS ANGELES	USA	10
4	GOYANG	SOUTH KOREA	8
=	TOKYO	JAPAN	8
6	INCHEON	SOUTH KOREA	5
7	HWASEONG	SOUTH KOREA	4
=	OSAKA	JAPAN	4
9	DALIAN	CHINA	3
=	GUANGZHOU	CHINA	3

TOP 10

BUILDINGS WITH THE HIGHEST HELIPADS

If you've got enough of a head for heights for a helicopter flight, these helipads will suit you fine...

	BUILDING	CITY	COUNTRY	YEAR COMPLETED	HELIPAD HEIGHT (M)	(FT)
1	GUANGZHOU INTERNATIONAL FINANCE CENTER	GUANGZHOU	CHINA	2010	438	1,437
2	CHINA WORLD TOWER	BEIJING	CHINA	2010	330	1,082.7
3	U.S. BANK TOWER	LOS ANGELES	USA	1990	310	1,017.1
4	NORTHEAST ASIA TRADE TOWER	INCHEON	SOUTH KOREA	2011	300	984.3
=	ABENO HARUKAS	OSAKA	JAPAN	2014	300	984.3
6	DOOSAN HAEUNDAE WE'VE THE ZENITH TOWER A	BUSAN	SOUTH KOREA	2011	299	981
7	LANDMARK TOWER	YOKOHAMA	JAPAN	1993	296	971.1
8	SEG PLAZA	SHENZHEN	CHINA	2000	292	958
9	UNITED INTERNATIONAL MANSION	CHONGQING	CHINA	2013	287	941.6
10	THREE INTERNATIONAL FINANCE CENTER	SEOUL	SOUTH KOREA	2012	284	931.7

The highest helipad in the world is on the Siachen glacier in the Himalayas:

20,997 FT

above sea level

CHINA WORLD TOWER

2 The 48th tallest building in the world is the third phase of Beijing's CWTC (China World Trade Center).

GUANGZHOU INTERNATIONAL FINANCE CENTER

1 This is the ninth tallest building in all of Asia. It houses a combination of office spaces and a hotel was built between 2006 and 2010.

HELIPAD CENTRAL

These countries have the highest ones...

- CHINA **4**
- SOUTH KOREA **3**
- JAPAN **2**
- USA **1**

TALLEST CONSTRUCTIONS

TALLEST TELECOM/ OBSERVATION TOWERS

Constructions like these need height to serve their purpose, and these are the highest in the world...

	BUILDING	COUNTRY	YEAR COMPLETED	HEIGHT (M)	(FT)
1	TOKYO SKY TREE	JAPAN	2012	634	2,080
2	CANTON TOWER	CHINA	2010	600	1,969
3	CN TOWER	CANADA	1976	553.3	1,815
4	OSTANKINO TOWER	RUSSIA	1967	540	1,772
5	ORIENTAL PEARL TELEVISION TOWER	CHINA	1995	468	1,535
6	MILAD TOWER	IRAN	2008	435	1,427
7	MENARA KUALA LUMPUR	MALAYSIA	1996	420.4	1,379
8	TIANJIN RADIO & TV TOWER	CHINA	1991	415.1	1,362
9	CENTRAL RADIO & TV TOWER	CHINA	1992	410.5	1,347
10	HENAN PROVINCE RADIO & TV TOWER	CHINA	2011	388	1,273

TOKYO SKY TREE

1 Although initially proposed in 2006, the construction of the Tokyo Sky Tree didn't begin until 2008. The tower has 13 elevators that can travel at 10 metres per second.

CANTON TOWER

2 It may not be the tallest construction in the world, but the Canton Tower is home to the world's highest post office, stationed 1,404.2 ft (428 m) up.

Menara Kuala Lumpur's total floors (above and below ground):

19

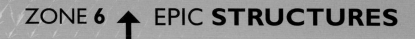

The tallest tower in Canada is the CN Tower:

1,815 FT

USA

3 The tallest tower in the United States is the Stratosphere Tower in Las Vegas. It extends 1,149 ft (350.2 m) up and has towered over the skyline since 1996.

TOP 10

COUNTRIES WITH THE MOST TELECOM TOWERS

The tallest towers are on the opposite page, and these are the nations home to the most...

	COUNTRY	NUMBER OF TELECOM TOWERS
1	THE NETHERLANDS	49
2	CHINA	25
3	USA	18
4	GERMANY	13
5	UK	7
6	CANADA	6
=	JAPAN	6
8	RUSSIA	4
9	ITALY	3
10	BELGIUM/GEORGIA/INDIA/SOUTH AFRICA/SOUTH KOREA/SPAIN	2

GERMANY

4 The Fernsehturm (aka the Berlin TV Tower) attracts 1.2 million visitors each year. Its antenna contributes to its 1,207.45 ft (368.03 m) height.

163

LONGEST DESIGNS

HANGZHOU BAY BRIDGE

9 Constructed over four years (2003–07), this gigantic bay-spanning bridge was carefully designed and planned for over a decade.

SPANNING TENS OF MILES

The number one actually exceeds 100 miles...

DANYANG–KUNSHAN GRAND BRIDGE 540,700 FT

TIANJIN GRAND BRIDGE 373,000 FT

WEINAN WEIHE GRAND BRIDGE 261,588 FT

BANG NA EXPRESSWAY 177,000 FT

BEIJING GRAND BRIDGE 157,982 FT

Tianjin Grand Bridge is over **70** MI long

LONGEST BRIDGES

TOP 10

Humans have been constructing bridges to connect places for centuries, but these are record breakers...

	BRIDGE	COUNTRY	LENGTH (M)	(FT)
1	DANYANG–KUNSHAN GRAND BRIDGE	CHINA	164,800	540,700
2	TIANJIN GRAND BRIDGE	CHINA	113,700	373,000
3	WEINAN WEIHE GRAND BRIDGE	CHINA	79,732	261,588
4	BANG NA EXPRESSWAY	THAILAND	54,000	177,000
5	BEIJING GRAND BRIDGE	CHINA	48,153	157,982
6	LAKE PONTCHARTRAIN CAUSEWAY	USA	38,442	126,122
7	MANCHAC SWAMP BRIDGE	USA	36,710	120,440
8	YANGCUN BRIDGE	CHINA	35,812	117,493
9	HANGZHOU BAY BRIDGE	CHINA	35,673	117,037
10	RUNYANG BRIDGE	CHINA	35,660	116,990

BANG NA EXPRESSWAY

4 This colossal bridge is 137.8 ft (42 m) wide. It is a toll bridge that required nearly 63,566,400 cubic ft (1.8 million cubic m) of concrete.

TOP 10

LONGEST ROLLER COASTERS

Theme park rides often feature twists and turns, but these coasters take you the greatest distances...

The Voyage ride lasts

2 MINS
45 SECS

	ROLLER COASTER	LOCATION	LENGTH (M)	(FT)
1	STEEL DRAGON 2000	NAGASHIMA SPA LAND (JAPAN)	2,479	8,133
2	THE ULTIMATE	LIGHTWATER VALLEY (UK)	2,268	7,442
3	THE BEAST	KINGS ISLAND (USA)	2,243	7,359
4	FUJIYAMA	FUJI-Q HIGHLAND (JAPAN)	2,045	6,709
5	FURY 325	CAROWINDS (USA)	2,012	6,602
6	MILLENNIUM FORCE	CEDAR POINT (USA)	2,010	6,595
7	FORMULA ROSSA	FERRARI WORLD (UNITED ARAB EMIRATES)	2,000	6,562
8	THE VOYAGE	HOLIDAY WORLD & SPLASHIN' SAFARI (USA)	1,964	6,442
9	CALIFORNIA SCREAMIN'	DISNEY CALIFORNIA ADVENTURE (USA)	1,851	6,072
10	DESPERADO	BUFFALO BILL'S (USA)	1,781	5,843

STEEL DRAGON 2000

1 Located in Mie Prefecture, Japan, this roller coaster gets its name from the fact that it was opened in the Year of the Dragon, 2000.

THE ULTIMATE

2 Situated in the North Yorkshire village of North Stainley, in the UK, this coaster ride is among 44 acres of woodland in the Lightwater Valley complex.

The Melbourne Star reopened with its new/second wheel:

DEC 23, 2013

HIGH ROLLER

1 This appropriately named ferris wheel, set in the heart of the gambling city of Las Vegas, was opened on March 31, 2014.

LONDON EYE

4 Open since March 2000, this iconic landmark on London's South Bank is the tallest ferris wheel in Europe. It features 32 passenger pods that can each hold 25 people.

TOP 10

BIGGEST FERRIS WHEELS

Providing spectacular views at great heights, these have become popular landmarks in many cities...

	FERRIS WHEEL	LOCATION	YEAR COMPLETED	HEIGHT (M)	(FT)
1	HIGH ROLLER	LAS VEGAS, NEVADA (USA)	2014	167.6	550
2	SINGAPORE FLYER	MARINA CENTRE (SINGAPORE)	2008	165	541
3	STAR OF NANCHANG	NANCHANG, JIANGXI (CHINA)	2006	160	525
4	LONDON EYE	SOUTH BANK, LONDON (UK)	2000	135	443
5	ORLANDO EYE	ORLANDO, FLORIDA (USA)	2015	122	400
6	SUZHOU FERRIS WHEEL	SUZHOU, JIANGSU (CHINA)	2009	120	394
=	MELBOURNE STAR	DOCKLANDS, MELBOURNE (AUSTRALIA)	2008	120	394
=	TIANJIN EYE	YONGLE BRIDGE, TIANJIN (CHINA)	2008	120	394
=	CHANGSHA FERRIS WHEEL	CHANGSHA, HUNAN (CHINA)	2004	120	394
=	ZHENGZHOU FERRIS WHEEL	CENTURY AMUSEMENT PARK, HENAN (CHINA)	2003	120	394

TOP 10

MOST POPULAR WATER PARKS

Have you visited any of these water parks? Take a close look at the annuals attendance figures...

	WATER PARK	LOCATION	ANNUAL ATTENDANCE
1	CHIMELONG WATER PARK	GUANGZHOU (CHINA)	2.26 MILLION
2	TYPHOON LAGOON (WALT DISNEY WORLD RESORT)	FLORIDA (USA)	2.19 MILLION
3	BLIZZARD BEACH (WALT DISNEY WORLD RESORT)	FLORIDA (USA)	2.01 MILLION
4	THERMAS DOS LARANJAIS	OLÍMPIA (BRAZIL)	1.94 MILLION
5	OCEAN WORLD	GANGWON-DO (SOUTH KOREA)	1.60 MILLION
6	AQUATICA	FLORIDA (USA)	1.57 MILLION
7	CARIBBEAN BAY (EVERLAND RESORT)	GYEONGGI-DO (SOUTH KOREA)	1.49 MILLION
8	AQUAVENTURE	DUBAI (UNITED ARAB EMIRATES)	1.4 MILLION
9	HOT PARK RIO QUENTE	CALDAS NOVAS (BRAZIL)	1.29 MILLION
10	WET 'N' WILD ORLANDO	FLORIDA (USA)	1.28 MILLION

AQUATICA

6 This water park includes two wave pools and 14 different slides, rides, and areas. There is also an 80,000-sq ft (7,432-sq m) constructed beach.

Wet 'n' Wild Orlando's total water slides: **17**

CHIMELONG WATER PARK

1 This water park has been operational for over ten years. Its neighbouring Chimelong Safari Park became home to giant panda offspring in 2014. The main Chimelong Paradise Park also has five roller coasters.

167

LEVIATHAN

10 Lasting 3 minutes 28 seconds, Leviathan has a drop height of 306 ft (93 m). Although it was the sixth Canadian roller coaster to be constructed, it is the country's fastest and tallest.

KINGDA KA

2 This roller coaster can carry 1,400 riders every hour, at speeds of 128 mph (206 kph). It has been open since May 21, 2005.

Superman: Escape From Krypton roller coaster height: **415** FT

TOP 10

FASTEST ROLLER COASTERS

For those of you that go on rides for the acceleration, these are the 10 you should seek out...

	ROLLER COASTER	LOCATION	TOP SPEED (KPH)	(MPH)
1	FORMULA ROSSA	FERRARI WORLD (UNITED ARAB EMIRATES)	240	149.1
2	KINGDA KA	SIX FLAGS GREAT ADVENTURE (USA)	206	128
3	TOP THRILL DRAGSTER	CEDAR POINT (USA)	193.1	120
4	DODONPA	FUJI-Q HIGHLAND (JAPAN)	172	106.9
5	SUPERMAN: ESCAPE FROM KRYPTON	SIX FLAGS MAGIC MOUNTAIN (USA)	162.2	100.8
6	TOWER OF TERROR II	DREAMWORLD (AUSTRALIA)	160.9	100
7	STEEL DRAGON 2000	NAGASHIMA SPA LAND (JAPAN)	152.9	95
=	FURY 325	CAROWINDS (USA)	152.9	95
9	MILLENNIUM FORCE	CEDAR POINT (USA)	149.7	93
10	LEVIATHAN	CANADA'S WONDERLAND (CANADA)	148.1	92

BIGGEST CINEMA SCREENS EVER

From temporary screens used for film events through to permanent IMAX cinemas, film fans should study this top 10...

	CINEMA SCREEN	LOCATION	TOTAL AREA (M²)	(FT²)
1	LOVELL RADIO TELESCOPE*	CHESHIRE (UK)	4,560.37	49,087
2	NOKIA N8*	MALMÖ (SWEDEN)	1,428	15,371
3	PINEWOOD STUDIOS*	MIDDLESEX (UK)	1,337.73	14,399
4	IMAX DARLING HARBOUR	SYDNEY (AUSTRALIA)	1,056.24	11,369
5	IMAX MELBOURNE	MELBOURNE (AUSTRALIA)	736	7,922.2
6	OSLO SPEKTRUM*	OSLO (NORWAY)	676	7,276.4
7	TOKYO DOME	TOKYO (JAPAN)	647	6,964.2
8	MEYDAN IMAX	DUBAI (UNITED ARAB EMIRATES)	638	6,867.4
=	PRASADS IMAX	HYDERABAD (INDIA)	638	6,867.4
10	KRUNGSRI IMAX	BANGKOK (THAILAND)	588	6,329.2

Temporary screen erected for one-night event.

TOP 5 BIGGEST IMAX SCREENS

Proving that IMAXs come in very different sizes...

IMAX DARLING HARBOUR
11,369 FT

IMAX MELBOURNE
7,922.2 FT

MEYDAN IMAX
6,867.4 FT

PRASADS IMAX
6,867.4 FT

KRUNGSRI IMAX
6,329.2 FT

Total IMAX cinema screens in the world:

1,000

KRUNGSRI IMAX

10 Located in Bangkok, the capital of Thailand, this huge cinema complex is part of a metropolis that contains 51 buildings that exceed 492 ft (150 m) in height.

LOVELL RADIO TELESCOPE

1 To celebrate the 50th anniversary of the telescope, this became a temporary cinema screen on October 5, 2007, showing astronomy and exploration films.

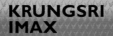

Preparation to construct Baku Crystal Hall began

AUG 2, 2011

SMART ARANETA COLISEUM

6 This huge arena is appropriately known as "The Big Dome". Although mainly home to basketball events, the 56-year-old venue also hosts music and religious events.

TOP 10

LARGEST INDOOR ARENAS

From rock and pop events to world-class sporting championships, these arenas have hosted them all...

	NAME	LOCATION	CAPACITY CROWD
1	PHILIPPINE ARENA	BOCAUE (PHILIPPINES)	55,000
2	SAITAMA SUPER ARENA	SAITAMA (JAPAN)	37,000
3	OLIMPIYSKIY	MOSCOW (RUSSIA)	35,000
4	GWANGMYEONG VELODROME	GWANGMYEONG (SOUTH KOREA)	30,000
5	TELENOR ARENA	BÆRUM (NORWAY)	26,000
6	KOMBANK ARENA	BELGRADE (SERBIA)	25,000
=	MINEIRINHO	BELO HORIZONTE (BRAZIL)	25,000
=	SMART ARANETA COLISEUM	QUEZON CITY (PHILIPPINES)	25,000
=	BAKU CRYSTAL HALL	BAKU (AZERBAIJAN)	25,000
=	SCC PETERBURGSKIY	ST PETERSBURG (RUSSIA)	25,000

SAITAMA SUPER ARENA

2 This Japanese arena was also the home to the official John Lennon Museum (2000–10). It featured a vast collection of personal items owned by Lennon's widow, artist Yoko Ono.

BIGGEST **STADIUMS**

When the demand for an event can fill the biggest arena a few times over, it's time to locate a stadium...

	NAME	LOCATION	CAPACITY CROWD
1	RUNGRADO 1ST OF MAY STADIUM	PYONGYANG (NORTH KOREA)	150,000
2	MICHIGAN STADIUM	MICHIGAN (USA)	107,601
3	BEAVER STADIUM	PENNSYLVANIA (USA)	107,572
4	OHIO STADIUM	OHIO (USA)	104,944
5	KYLE FIELD	TEXAS (USA)	102,512
6	NEYLAND STADIUM	TENNESSEE (USA)	102,455
7	TIGER STADIUM	LOUISIANA (USA)	102,321
8	BRYANT-DENNY STADIUM	ALABAMA (USA)	101,821
9	DARRELL K ROYAL-TEXAS MEMORIAL STADIUM	TEXAS (USA)	100,119
10	MELBOURNE CRICKET GROUND	MELBOURNE (AUSTRALIA)	100,024

BEAVER STADIUM

3 Not an animal connection, this stadium is actually named after former Pennsylvania governor James A. Beaver.

MELBOURNE CRICKET GROUND

10 This has been the home of the world-famous MCC (Melbourne Cricket Club) since the1850s, with the first match played on September 30, 1854.

Louisiana's Tiger Stadium first opened in **1924**

171

RIO DE JANEIRO

1 The swirling orange and yellow logo of the 2016 Summer Paralympics was revealed on November 26, 2011, nearly five years before the Games.

TOP 10

MOST RECENT 10 PARALYMPICS

These were the locations and calendar dates of the 2016 Paralympic Games and prior nine...

	HOST CITY	COUNTRY	KNOWN AS	GAMES' PERIOD	YEAR
1	**RIO DE JANEIRO**	BRAZIL	XV PARALYMPIC GAMES	SEP 7–18	**2016**
2	**SOCHI**	RUSSIA	XI PARALYMPIC WINTER GAMES	MAR 7–16	**2014**
3	**LONDON**	UK	XIV PARALYMPIC GAMES	AUG 29–SEP 9	**2012**
4	**VANCOUVER**	CANADA	X PARALYMPIC WINTER GAMES	MAR 12–21	**2010**
5	**BEIJING**	CHINA	XIII PARALYMPIC GAMES	SEP 6–17	**2008**
6	**TURIN**	ITALY	IX PARALYMPIC WINTER GAMES	MAR 10–19	**2006**
7	**ATHENS**	GREECE	XII PARALYMPIC GAMES	SEP 17–28	**2004**
8	**SALT LAKE CITY**	USA	VIII PARALYMPIC WINTER GAMES	MAR 7–16	**2002**
9	**SYDNEY**	AUSTRALIA	XI PARALYMPIC GAMES	OCT 18–29	**2000**
10	**NAGANO**	JAPAN	VII PARALYMPIC WINTER GAMES	MAR 5–14	**1998**

VANCOUVER

4 506 athletes took part from 44 countries. The main stadium was BC Place in False Creek, which was first officially opened in 1983.

VII Paralympic Winter Games in Nagano, Japan featured

122

events

183

GRAPH OF OLYMPIC COSTS

Here's how the 5 most expensive compare visually...

SOCHI
$51 BILLION

BEIJING
$44 BILLION

LONDON
$14.6 BILLION

RIO
$9.82 BILLION

BARCELONA
$9.3 BILLION

SOCHI

1 These Games featured 98 events, compared to Moscow's 203 in its Summer Games in 1980. Mario & Sonic at the Sochi 2014 Olympic Winter Games was released for the Wii U in November 2013.

The 2008 Olympics in Beijing, China featured

28

different sporting disciplines

TOP 10

MOST EXPENSIVE OLYMPIC BUDGETS

Being a host nation is a prestigious event, but it also comes with an expensive bill...

	HOST CITY	COUNTRY	YEAR	EST. TOTAL BUDGET ($ BILLIONS)
1	SOCHI	RUSSIA	2014	51
2	BEIJING	CHINA	2008	44
3	LONDON	UK	2012	14.6
4	RIO DE JANEIRO	BRAZIL	2016	9.82
5	BARCELONA	SPAIN	1992	9.3
6	ATHENS	GREECE	2004	9
7	SYDNEY	AUSTRALIA	2000	6.6
8	VANCOUVER	CANADA	2010	6.4
9	MOSCOW	SOVIET UNION (NOW RUSSIA)	1980	1.35
10	SALT LAKE CITY	USA	2002	1.2

2 Of the 86 countries that participated at these Summer Olympics, 43 world records were achieved. China won the most gold medals at the games, 51 in total.

MOST HOSTED OLYMPIC & PARALYMPIC NATIONS

These countries have hosted Games more than any others...

	COUNTRY	TOTAL TIMES OLYMPIC & PARALYMPIC GAMES
1	USA	11
2	FRANCE	6
3	CANADA	5
=	ITALY	5
=	JAPAN	5
=	UK	5
7	AUSTRIA	4
=	GERMANY	4
=	GREECE	4
=	NORWAY	4

FRANCE

2 France hosted Games in 1900 (Summer Olympics), 1924 (Summer and Winter Olympics), 1968 (Winter Olympics), and 1992 (Winter Olympics and Winter Paralympics).

France's total medals from all the Paralympic Games (before Rio 2016): **1,148**

BRAZIL

Rio de Janeiro's 2016 Summer Olympics marks the first time any South American country has hosted any form of the Games.

Florence Griffith Joyner's 100m record has remained unbeaten for over

28

years

KERRON STEWART

7

Born in Kingston, the capital of Jamaica, Stewart has amassed 26 career medals. Her three world championship golds include the 4 x 100 m relay at Beijing in 2015.

CHRISTINE ARRON

5

Now retired, the French runner achieved the 4 x 100 m relay gold medal at the 2003 World Championships in Athletics held in Paris.

TOP 10

FASTEST 100 m FEMALE SPRINTERS

This chart reveals the 10 fastest women of all time, plus their average speed...

	NAME	COUNTRY	YEAR	TIME (SECS)	AVERAGE SPEED (KPH)	(MPH)
1	FLORENCE GRIFFITH JOYNER	USA	1988	10.49	34.31	21.32
2	CARMELITA JETER	USA	2009	10.64	33.83	21.02
3	MARION JONES	USA	1998	10.65	33.80	21.00
4	SHELLY-ANN FRASER-PRYCE	JAMAICA	2012	10.70	33.65	20.91
5	CHRISTINE ARRON	FRANCE	1998	10.73	33.56	20.85
6	MERLENE OTTEY	JAMAICA	1996	10.74	33.52	20.83
7	KERRON STEWART	JAMAICA	2009	10.75	33.49	20.81
8	EVELYN ASHFORD	USA	1984	10.76	33.46	20.79
=	VERONICA CAMPBELL-BROWN	JAMAICA	2011	10.76	33.46	20.79
10	IRINA PRIVALOVA/IVET LALOVA-COLLIO	RUSSIA/BULGARIA	1994/2004	10.77	33.43	20.77

JUSTIN GATLIN

5 34-year-old Gatlin's new personal best in the chart below was achieved at the Qatar Athletic Super Grand Prix on May 15, 2015.

Usain Bolt, the fastest man on Earth, is **6 FT 5 IN** tall

TOP 10

FASTEST 100 M MALE SPRINTERS

Recall how fast it feels to travel 30 mph (48 kph) in a car, and then see how fast these men can move...

	NAME	COUNTRY	YEAR	TIME (SECS)	AVERAGE SPEED (KPH)	(MPH)
1	USAIN BOLT	JAMAICA	2009	9.58	37.58	23.35
2	TYSON GAY	USA	2009	9.69	37.14	23.08
=	YOHAN BLAKE	JAMAICA	2012	9.69	37.14	23.08
4	ASAFA POWELL	JAMAICA	2008	9.72	37.03	23.01
5	JUSTIN GATLIN	USA	2014	9.74	36.85	22.90
6	NESTA CARTER	JAMAICA	2010	9.78	36.81	22.87
7	MAURICE GREENE	USA	1999	9.79	36.77	22.85
8	STEVE MULLINGS	JAMAICA	2011	9.80	36.74	22.83
9	RICHARD THOMPSON	TRINIDAD AND TOBAGO	2014	9.82	36.66	22.78
10	DONOVAN BAILEY/BRUNY SURIN/TRAYVON BROMWELL	CANADA/CANADA/USA	1996/1999/2015	9.84	36.58	22.73

ASAFA POWELL

4 Although he is currently the fourth fastest man on Earth, Powell held the world record for the 100 m for nearly three years between 2005 and 2008.

SPEED MASTERS

FLORENCE GRIFFITH JOYNER

1 Flo-Jo's career included four gold and three silver medals, won between 1984 and 1987. She sadly passed away in her sleep on September 21, 1998.

JARMILA KRATOCHVÍLOVÁ

4 The Czech athlete's world record for the 800 m has not been bested in 33 years. Between 1980 and 1983, Kratochvílová won five gold medals in 400 m and 800 m.

TOP 10

QUICKEST SPORTSWOMEN

Focusing on 10 sports that require explosive bursts of acceleration, these are their 10 fastest women...

	SPORT	DISTANCE	FASTEST PERSON	COUNTRY	YEAR	TIME	AVERAGE SPEED (KPH)	(MPH)
1	RUNNING	100 M	FLORENCE GRIFFITH JOYNER	USA	1988	0:10.49	34.32	21.32
2	RUNNING	200 M	FLORENCE GRIFFITH JOYNER	USA	1988	0:21.34	33.74	20.96
3	RUNNING	400 M	MARITA KOCH	GERMANY	1985	0:47.60	30.25	18.8
4	RUNNING	800 M	JARMILA KRATOCHVÍLOVÁ	CZECH REPUBLIC	1983	1:53.28	25.42	15.8
5	SWIMMING: FREESTYLE	50 M	RANOMI KROMOWIDJOJO	NETHERLANDS	2013	0:23.24	7.74	4.81
6	SWIMMING: BUTTERFLY	50 M	THERESE ALSHAMMAR	SWEDEN	2009	0:24.38	7.39	4.59
7	SWIMMING: FREESTYLE	100 M	LIBBY TRICKETT	AUSTRALIA	2009	0:51.01	7.07	4.39
8	SWIMMING: BACKSTROKE	50 M	ETIENE MEDEIROS	BRAZIL	2014	0:25.67	7.02	4.36
9	SWIMMING: BUTTERFLY	100 M	SARAH SJÖSTRÖM	SWEDEN	2014	0:54.61	6.59	4.1
10	SWIMMING: FREESTYLE	200 M	SARAH SJÖSTRÖM	SWEDEN	2014	1:50.78	6.5	4.04

5–10 performed in Short Course (25 m) pools.

LIBBY TRICKETT

7 The world record-holder in 100 m freestyle picked up her first international individual medal, a bronze, at the 2003 World Championships.

Therese Alshammar was born
AUG 26, 1977

TATYANA MCFADDEN

3

Russian-born USA athlete Tatyana McFadden, 27, won three gold medals at the Summer Olympics in 2012.

TOP 10

QUICKEST FEMALE PARALYMPIANS

This is not a definitive Top 10 because comparing the different classes is unfair. This chart merely shows the fastest speeds achieved in each "sprint" event...

	SPORT	DISTANCE	FASTEST PERSON	CLASS	COUNTRY	YEAR	TIME	AVERAGE SPEED (KPH)	(MPH)
1	**RUNNING**	100 M	OMARA DURAND	T12	CUBA	2015	**0:11.65**	**31.58**	**19.62**
2	**RUNNING**	200 M	OMARA DURAND	T13	CUBA	2015	**0:23.67**	**30.42**	**18.9**
3	**RUNNING**	800 M	TATYANA MCFADDEN	T54	USA	2015	**1:42.72**	**28.03**	**17.42**
4	**RUNNING**	400 M	TATYANA MCFADDEN	T54	USA	2015	**0:51.90**	**27.75**	**17.24**
5	**SWIMMING: FREESTYLE**	50 M	OXANA SAVCHENKO	S12	RUSSIA	2009	**0:26.54**	**6.78**	**4.21**
6	**SWIMMING: BUTTERFLY**	50 M	SOPHIE PASCOE	S10	NEW ZEALAND	2013	**0:29.08**	**6.19**	**3.85**
7	**SWIMMING: FREESTYLE**	100 M	OXANA SAVCHENKO	S12	RUSSIA	2009	**0:58.60**	**6.14**	**3.82**
8	**SWIMMING: BACKSTROKE**	50 M	SOPHIE PASCOE	S10	NEW ZEALAND	2013	**0:30.49**	**5.9**	**3.67**
9	**SWIMMING: FREESTYLE**	200 M	VALÉRIE GRAND'MAISON	S13	CANADA	2008	**2:08.53**	**5.6**	**3.48**
10	**SWIMMING: BUTTERFLY**	100 M	JOANNA MENDAK	S12	POLAND	2009	**1:05.10**	**5.53**	**3.44**

5–10 performed in Short Course (25 m) pools.

Joanna Mendak's total Paralympics Games' medals:

6

QUICKEST COUNTRIES

Here's how the above chart looks ranked by nation...

- CUBA **2**
- USA **2**
- RUSSIA **2**
- NEW ZEALAND **2**
- CANADA **1**
- POLAND **1**

FLORENT MANAUDOU

5 6.5-ft (1.96-m) tall French swimmer achieved his two world records at the 2014 FINA World Swimming Championships, held in Doha, Qatar between December 3–7.

MICHAEL JOHNSON

3 This sprinter achieved eight gold medals during international competitions between 1991 and 2000. These include four Olympic golds.

TOP 10

QUICKEST SPORTSMEN

These are the 10 fastest men from the sports that involve fast acceleration...

	SPORT	DISTANCE	FASTEST PERSON	COUNTRY	YEAR	TIME	AVERAGE SPEED (KPH)	(MPH)
1	RUNNING	100 M	USAIN BOLT	JAMAICA	2009	0:09.58	37.58	23.35
2	RUNNING	200 M	USAIN BOLT	JAMAICA	2009	0:19.19	37.52	23.31
3	RUNNING	400 M	MICHAEL JOHNSON	USA	1999	0:43.18	33.35	20.72
4	RUNNING	800 M	DAVID RUDISHA	KENYA	2012	1:40.91	28.54	17.73
5	SWIMMING: FREESTYLE	50 M	FLORENT MANAUDOU	FRANCE	2014	0:20.26	8.88	5.52
6	SWIMMING: BUTTERFLY	50 M	STEFFEN DEIBLER	GERMANY	2009	0:21.80	8.26	5.13
7	SWIMMING: BACKSTROKE	50 M	FLORENT MANAUDOU	UK	2014	0:22.22	8.1	5.03
8	SWIMMING: FREESTYLE	100 M	AMAURY LEVEAUX	FRANCE	2008	0:44.94	8.01	4.98
9	SWIMMING: BUTTERFLY	100 M	CHAD LE CLOS	SOUTH AFRICA	2014	0:48.44	7.44	4.62
10	SWIMMING: FREESTYLE	200 M	PAUL BIEDERMANN	GERMANY	2009	1:39.37	7.26	4.51

5–10 performed in Short Course (25 m) pools.

Chad le Clos holds **2** world records for 100 m and 200 m butterfly

QUICKEST MALE PARALYMPIANS

Although not a definitive chart, because comparing classifications is unfair, this Top 10 reveals the fastest speeds achieved in the "sprint" sports...

	SPORT	DISTANCE	FASTEST PERSON	CLASS	COUNTRY	YEAR	TIME	AVERAGE SPEED (KPH)	(MPH)
1	RUNNING	200 M	ALAN FONTELES CARDOSO OLIVEIRA	T43	BRAZIL	2013	0:20.66	34.85	21.65
2	RUNNING	100 M	JASON SMYTH	T13	IRELAND	2012	0:10.46	34.42	21.39
3	RUNNING	400 M	LIXIN ZHANG	T54	CHINA	2008	0:45.07	31.95	19.85
4	RUNNING	800 M	MARCEL HUG	T54	SWITZERLAND	2010	1:31.12	31.61	19.64
5	SWIMMING: FREESTYLE	50 M	ANDRE BRASIL	S10	BRAZIL	2009	0:22.44	8.02	4.98
6	SWIMMING: FREESTYLE	100 M	ANDRE BRASIL	S10	BRAZIL	2009	0:48.70	7.39	4.59
7	SWIMMING: BUTTERFLY	50 M	TIMOTHY ANTALFY	S13	AUSTRALIA	2014	0:24.60	7.32	4.55
8	SWIMMING: BACKSTROKE	50 M	SEAN RUSSO	S13	AUSTRALIA	2013	0:27.30	6.59	4.1
9	SWIMMING: BUTTERFLY	100 M	ANDRE BRASIL	S10	BRAZIL	2009	0:54.76	6.57	4.08
10	SWIMMING: FREESTYLE	200 M	PHILIPPE GAGNON	S10	CANADA	2002	1:52.83	6.38	3.97

5–10 performed in Short Course (25 m) pools.

LIXIN ZHANG

3 The Chinese Paralympian won four gold medals at the 2008 Summer Paralympics held in Beijing. He won an additional gold medal at the London 2012 Paralympics.

Philippe Gagnon's total medals at the 2000 Paralympics: **4** (3 gold, 1 silver)

ALAN FONTELES CARDOSO OLIVEIRA

1 Born on August 21, 1992, Oliveira has already won four gold, four silver, and four bronze medals from Paralympic Games and world championships.

CALE YARBOROUGH

9 His career also included 60 pole positions over 33 years of NASCAR competitions. His first NASCAR race was in his home state at the Bojangles Southern 500 in 1957.

Rusty Wallace's total pole positions: **36**

GREATEST NASCAR CHAMPIONS' TOTAL RACES

Of all the championship NASCAR events, these drivers took part in the most...

	NAME	FROM	CAREER RACES
1	RICHARD PETTY	NORTH CAROLINA, USA	1,199
2	DARRELL WALTRIP	KENTUCKY, USA	921
3	JEFF GORDON	CALIFORNIA, USA	865
4	DALE EARNHARDT	NORTH CAROLINA, USA	812
5	BOBBY ALLISON	FLORIDA, USA	778
6	RUSTY WALLACE	MISSOURI, USA	749
7	JIMMIE JOHNSON	CALIFORNIA, USA	596
8	DAVID PEARSON	SOUTH CAROLINA, USA	583
9	CALE YARBOROUGH	SOUTH CAROLINA, USA	568
10	LEE PETTY	NORTH CAROLINA, USA	427

DARRELL WALTRIP

2 These days, the former NASCAR champion is a broadcaster. He is Fox's lead race commentator, alongside veteran announcer Mike Joy and NASCAR driver Jeff Gordon.

F1 CONSTUCTOR NATIONS

Here's the below chart summarized by country...

UK
33

ITALY
16

AUSTRIA
4

FRANCE
3

GERMANY
2

Renault
has been involved
with F1 racing since
1977

MCLAREN

3 New Zealand engineer and car designer Bruce McLaren set up this company in 1963. Sadly, he died from a car accident in 1970, aged 32.

TOP 10

MOST SUCCESSFUL F1 CONSTRUCTORS

These are the engineering brains behind F1's most world championship wins...

FERRARI

1 This company began as Scuderia Ferrari in 1929. Ferrari is the only team that has participated in every F1 world championship.

NAME	COUNTRY	TOTAL WORLD CONSTRUCTORS CHAMPIONSHIP WINS
1 FERRARI	ITALY	16
2 WILLIAMS	UK	9
3 MCLAREN	UK	8
4 LOTUS	UK	7
5 RED BULL	AUSTRIA	4
6 COOPER	UK	2
= BRABHAM	UK	2
= RENAULT	FRANCE	2
= MERCEDES	GERMANY	2
10 MATRA/VANWELL, BRM, TYRELL, BENETTON & BRAWN	FRANCE/UK	1*

* Each team at the 10th spot has won one World Constructor Championship.

MIKE HAILWOOD

4

British biking legend Mike Hailwood also achieved 79 fastest laps. In the Sixties and Seventies, he also had a Formula One career and raced in 50 Grand Prix events.

CASEY STONER

10 Choosing to retire from the sport in 2012 at age 27, Stoner notched up 39 pole positions during his six-year career. Then, in 2015, the Australian decided to return to the sport.

Giacomo Agostini's wins include **68** in the 500cc class

GRAND PRIX MOTORCYCLE MASTERS

TOP 10

These are the 10 bikers who have notched up more wins than their fellow riders...

NAME	COUNTRY	TOTAL WINS
1 GIACOMO AGOSTINI	ITALY	122
2 VALENTINO ROSSI	ITALY	112
3 ÁNGEL NIETO	SPAIN	90
4 MIKE HAILWOOD	UK	76
5 JORGE LORENZO	SPAIN	60
6 MICHAEL DOOHAN	AUSTRALIA	54
7 PHIL READ	UK	52
8 DANI PEDROSA	SPAIN	50
= MARC MÁRQUEZ	SPAIN	50
10 CASEY STONER/JIM REDMAN	AUSTRALIA/ RHODESIA	45

GIACOMO AGOSTINI

1 Known by his nickname of "Ago", in addition to his Grand Prix wins at the top of this chart, Agostini also triumphed at 15 MotorcycleWorld Championships.

TOP 10

MOST SUCCESSFUL MOTOCROSS NATIONS

Off-road motorcycle racing involves high speeds, leaps, and a lot of dirt...

	COUNTRY	TOTAL WORLD CHAMPIONSHIPS MEDALS
1	BELGIUM	135
2	SWEDEN	55
3	UK	47
4	ITALY	45
5	FRANCE	43
6	NETHERLANDS	36
7	USA	25
8	GERMANY	24
9	FINLAND	14
10	CZECH REPUBLIC	12

Stefan Everts has won the most World Championships:

10

RYAN DUNGEY

By the age of 24, American Ryan Dungey had already won every title the various Motocross events had to offer. Before his 25th birthday, he notched up 146 AMA Motocross/Supercross wins.

BELGIUM

1 The popularity of Motocross means Belgium has 13 courses available for training and racing. Retired Belgian rider Stefan Everts won 10 world titles.

The Mongol Derby began in **2009**

FIVE FURTHEST CHALLENGES

Here's how the top 5 compare graphically...

| TOUR DE FRANCE 3,569.8 MI | GREAT DIVIDE MOUNTAIN BIKE ROUTE 2,745 MI | FREEDOM TRAIL CHALLENGE 1,460.2 MI | ULTRAMARATHON 1,000+ MI | YUKON QUEST 1,000 MI |

TOP 10

LONGEST ENDURANCE SPORT EVENTS

These are the sports that push human stamina to its limit and way beyond...

	NAME	EVENTS INCLUDED	TOTAL DISTANCE COVERED (KM)	(MI)
1	**TOUR DE FRANCE^**	CYCLING	**5,745***	**3,569.8***
2	**GREAT DIVIDE MOUNTAIN BIKE ROUTE**	MOUNTAIN BIKING	**4,418***	**2,745***
3	**FREEDOM TRAIL CHALLENGE**	MOUNTAIN BIKING	**2,350***	**1,460.2***
4	**ULTRAMARATHON**	RUNNING, WALKING	**1,609+***	**1,000+***
5	**YUKON QUEST**	DOG SLEDDING	**1,609**	**1,000***
6	**MONGOL DERBY**	HORSE RIDING	**1,000****	**621.37****
7	**IRON MAN TRIATHALON**	SWIMMING (2.3 MI), CYCLING (112 MI), MARATHON (26.2 MI)	**226.31**	**140.6**
8	**POWERMAN ZOFINGEN DUATHALON**	HILL RUN (6.2 MI), HILL CYCLE (93.2 MI), HILL RUN (18.6 MI)	**190**	**118.06**
9	**CANADIAN SKI MARATHON**	SKIING	**160**	**99.42**
10	**QUADRATHALON**	SWIMMING (42.48 MI), KAYAKING (12.4 MI), CYCLING (62.1 MI), RUNNING (13 MI)	**145**	**90.1**

^ *Longest ever Tour de France, staged in 1926.*   * *Multi-day event.*   ** *Multiple horses used.*

TOUR DE FRANCE

1

The first ever Tour de France, staged July 1–19, 1903, was won by Maurice-Francois Garin. The course covered 1,509 mi (2,428 km) across six stages.

EKTRISCHE BMW i3

WILSON KIPSANG

3 At the 2014 London Marathon, Kipsang came in first place with in a new course record of 2 hours 4 minutes and 29 seconds.

TOP 10

FASTEST MALE & FEMALE MARATHON RUNNERS

These 10 men and women are the masters of endurance racing...

	NAME	SEX	COUNTRY	YEAR	TIME	AVERAGE SPEED (KPH)	(MPH)
1	DENNIS KIPRUTO KIMETTO	MALE	KENYA	2014	2:02.57	20.58	12.79
2	EMMANUEL MUTAI	MALE	KENYA	2014	2:03.13	20.55	12.77
▶ 3	WILSON KIPSANG	MALE	KENYA	2013	2:03.23	20.52	12.75
4	PATRICK MAKAU	MALE	KENYA	2011	2:03.38	20.47	12.72
5	HAILE GEBRSELASSIE	MALE	ETHIOPIA	2008	2:03.59	20.42	12.69
▶ 6	PAULA RADCLIFFE	FEMALE	UK	2003	2:15.25	18.70	11.62
7	MARY KEITANY	FEMALE	KENYA	2012	2:18.37	18.30	11.37
8	CATHERINE NDEREBA	FEMALE	KENYA	2001	2:18.47	18.28	11.36
9	TIKI GELANA	FEMALE	ETHIOPIA	2012	2:18.58	18.27	11.35
=	MIZUKI NOGUCHI	FEMALE	JAPAN	2005	2:19.12	18.20	11.31

PAULA RADCLIFFE

6 Paula Radcliffe retired in April 2015, after taking part in the London Marathon on April 26, 2015. Her career medals include 15 gold.

Tiki Gelana won the gold medal for the marathon at the

2012

Olympics

GOING THE DISTANCE

TOP 10

LONGEST LONG JUMPS

These 10 athletes have leapt the greatest distances into a soft sand pit landing...

	ATHLETE	COUNTRY	YEAR	DISTANCE (M)	(FT)
1	MIKE POWELL	USA	1991	8.95	29.36
2	BOB BEAMON	USA	1968	8.9	29.20
3	CARL LEWIS	USA	1991	8.87	29.10
4	ROBERT EMMIYAN	USSR (NOW RUSSIA)	1987	8.86	29.06
5	LARRY MYRICKS	USA	1988	8.74	28.67
=	ERICK WALDER	USA	1994	8.74	28.67
=	DWIGHT PHILLIPS	USA	2009	8.74	28.67
8	IRVING SALADINO	PANAMA	2008	8.73	28.64
9	IVÁN PEDROSO	CUBA	1995	8.71	28.58
=	SEBASTIAN BAYER	GERMANY	2009	8.71	28.58

Irving Saladino was born on **JAN 23, 1983**

GALINA CHISTYAKOVA

Russian Galina Chistyakova may not be part of this Top 10, but she holds the unbeaten female long jump record. Her 24.67 ft (7.52 m) jump was achieved on June 11, 1988.

SEBASTIAN BAYER

9 Born in Aachen, Germany on June 11, 1986, Bayer's distance on this chart is the second longest jump for indoor competition. He has also won three European Championships.

MIKE POWELL

1 His record was achieved at the World Championships in Athletics held in Tokyo, Japan, in 1991. Powell also won two silver long jump Olympic medals, in 1988 and 1992.

SPORTS THAT PROPEL THE BALL THE FURTHEST

TOP 10

For all the sports where a ball is thrown/hit, these are the all-time ball distance records...

	SPORT	CHAMPION	COUNTRY	YEAR	DISTANCE (M)	(FT)
1	LONG DRIVE GOLF	MIKE DOBBYN	USA	2007	503.83	1,653
2	PGA GOLF	MIKE AUSTIN	USA	1974	471	1,545.3
3	BASEBALL (HOME RUN)	MICKEY MANTLE	USA	1960	193.24	634
4	CRICKET (HIT/SIX)	SHAHID KHAN AFRIDI	PAKISTAN	2013	158	518.37
5	BASEBALL (THROW)	GLEN GORBOUS	CANADA	1957	135.89	445.83
6	CRICKET (THROW)	ROALD BRADSTOCK	UK	2010	132.6	435.04
7	SOCCER (GOAL)	ASMIR BEGOVIĆ	BOSNIA	2013	91.9	301.5
8	RUGBY	GERRY BRAND	SOUTH AFRICA	1932	77.7	254.92
9	FOOTBALL (FIELD GOAL)	CHING DO KIM	USA	1944	71.32	234
10	SOCCER (THROW IN)	THOMAS GRONNEMARK	DENMARK	2010	51.33	168.4

MIKE DOBBYN

1 This American Long Drive Golf professional is 6.7 ft (2.01 m) tall. The World Long Drive Championship has been held annually since 1975.

ASMIR BEGOVIĆ

7 Born in Bosnia and Herzegovina, the Chelsea goalkeeper's recording-breaking goal was scored against Southampton FC while he played for Stoke City (2010–15).

Shahid Khan Afridi's total number of sixes struck:

351

Paris Saint-Germain FC has been a soccer club for over **46** years

MOST POPULAR TEAMS ON FACEBOOK

TOP 10

In terms of "Likes", these are the sports teams that have the most fans...

	TEAM	SPORT	"LIKES" (MILLIONS)
1	FC BARCELONA	SOCCER	87.3
2	REAL MADRID CF	SOCCER	84.8
3	MANCHESTER UNITED FC	SOCCER	66.7
4	CHELSEA FC	SOCCER	43.7
5	ARSENAL FC	SOCCER	33.7
6	FC BAYERN MÜNCHEN	SOCCER	32.7
7	LIVERPOOL FC	SOCCER	26.4
8	AC MILAN	SOCCER	24.5
9	PARIS SAINT-GERMAIN FC	SOCCER	21.3
10	LA LAKERS	BASKETBALL	21.2

FIVE SOCCER GIANTS

Here's how the top 5 compare visually...

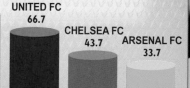

FC BARCELONA 87.3

REAL MADRID CF 84.8

MANCHESTER UNITED FC 66.7

CHELSEA FC 43.7

ARSENAL FC 33.7

FC BARCELONA

1 Its stadium, Camp Nou, can hold 99,354 people. Lionel Messi holds several records for the club, including the most goals scored at 447.

LA LAKERS

10 The LA Lakers has won the most consecutive games. The 33 wins occurred between Nov 5, 1971 and Jan 9, 1972.

MIAMI HEAT

8 Founded in 1988, current coach Erik Spoelstra has been with them since 2008. He is the sixth the team has had.

MOST POPULAR TEAMS ON TWITTER

TOP 10

On the social media micro-blog platform, these teams have the most followers...

	TEAM	SPORT	FOLLOWERS (MILLIONS)
1	REAL MADRID CF	SOCCER	17.3
2	FC BARCELONA	SOCCER	16.1
3	ARSENAL FC	SOCCER	6.4
4	MANCHESTER UNITED FC	SOCCER	6.2
5	CHELSEA FC	SOCCER	6.1
6	LIVERPOOL FC	SOCCER	4.9
7	LA LAKERS	BASKETBALL	4.5
8	MIAMI HEAT	BASKETBALL	3.1
9	AC MILAN	SOCCER	2.9
10	MANCHESTER CITY FC	SOCCER	2.7

ARSENAL FC

3 This British soccer team dates back 130 years to 1886. Its global fanbase means Arsenal is valued at more than $1 billion. Its Emirates Stadium home has 152 executive suites.

Real Madrid CF was founded over a century ago on **MAR 6, 1902**

201

MUSIC

ZONE **8**

Apolog

MOST DOWNLOADED SONGS EVER

TOP 10

Digital music sales have contributed to the overall success of singles and albums for over a decade...

	ARTIST(S)	SONG	YEAR RELEASED	TOTAL DOWNLOADS
1	THE BLACK EYED PEAS	I GOTTA FEELING	2009	8,770,000
2	ADELE	ROLLING IN THE DEEP	2010	8,508,000
3	LMFAO FT. LAUREN BENNETT & GOONROCK	PARTY ROCK ANTHEM	2001	8,096,000
4	GOTYE FT. KIMBRA	SOMEBODY THAT I USED TO KNOW	2011	7,941,000
5	IMAGINE DRAGONS	RADIOACTIVE	2012	7,902,000
6	MACKLEMORE & RYAN LEWIS FT. WANZ	THRIFT SHOP	2012	7,842,000
7	CARLY RAE JEPSEN	CALL ME MAYBE	2011	7,632,000
8	ROBIN THICKE FT. T.I. & PHARRELL	BLURRED LINES	2013	7,486,000
9	FLORIDA GEORGIA LINE	CRUISE	2012	7,440,000
10	FLO RIDA FT. T-PAIN	LOW	2007	7,297,000

CARLY RAE JEPSEN

7 The Canadian singer-songwriter drafted in Oscar-winning actor Tom Hanks to star in the music video for her 2015 single "I Really Like You" (taken from her third album, E•MO•TION).

Total digital tracks sold in 2015
964.8 MILLION

BY THE NUMBERS

Here's the above chart but expressed by types of artists...

SOLO ARTIST 2
COLLABORATIONS 5
BANDS 3

ADELE

2 "Hello" (the first single from the 2015 album 25) has been played on US radio shows more than 270,000 times, creating in excess of 1.56 billion audience impressions.

204

BEYONCÉ

8 The Super Bowl 50 halftime show (Feb 7, 2016) saw Beyoncé perform alongside Coldplay and Bruno Mars. She also headlined the halftime show on Feb 3, 2013.

TAYLOR SWIFT

3 The Pennsylvania, USA-born singer-songwriter has won 248 international awards, including 22 Billboard Music Awards. She has played the guitar since she was 12 years old.

In its first week on sale, Adele's 25 was downloaded **1.1 MILLION** times

MOST DOWNLOADED ALBUMS EVER

TOP 10

From Apple iTunes and Amazon to Tidal and Bandcamp, there are numerous websites that sell digital albums...

	ARTIST(S)	SONG	YEAR RELEASED	TOTAL DOWNLOADS
1	ADELE	21	2011	3,225,000
2	ADELE	25	2015	2,466,000
3	TAYLOR SWIFT	1989	2014	2,369,000
4	MUMFORD & SONS	SIGH NO MORE	2009	1,776,000
5	IMAGINE DRAGONS	NIGHT VISIONS	2012	1,588,000
6	VARIOUS	FROZEN (ORIGINAL SOUNDTRACK)	2013	1,566,000
7	MUMFORD & SONS	BABEL	2012	1,453,000
8	BEYONCÉ	BEYONCÉ	2013	1,440,000
9	EMINEM	RECOVERY	2010	1,394,000
10	TAYLOR SWIFT	RED	2012	1,279,000

Between 2014—15, music streaming increased **92.8%**

FETTY WAP

1 His debut single "Trap Queen" reached the number two position on the US's Billboard Hot 100 in May 2015. His self-titled 17-track debut album featured guest performances by Monty and M80.

MAJOR LAZER & DJ SNAKE FT. M

5 "Lean On" was taken from Major Lazer's third album *Peace Is The Mission* (released June 1, 2015). DJ Snake is French producer William Grigahcine, and MØ is Danish singer-songwriter Karen Marie Ørsted.

TOP 10

MOST ON-DEMAND STREAMED SONGS 2015

Streaming as a way of experiencing music was more popular than ever in 2015. These are the songs that were played the most...

	ARTIST(S)	SONG	TOTAL ON-DEMAND AUDIO STREAMS
1	FETTY WAP	TRAP QUEEN	214,842,000
2	THE WEEKND	THE HILLS	207,504,000
3	DRAKE	HOTLINE BLING	177,413,000
4	THE WEEKND	CAN'T FEEL MY FACE	174,451,000
5	MAJOR LAZER & DJ SNAKE FT. MØ	LEAN ON	167,819,000
6	MARK RONSON FT. BRUNO MARS	UPTOWN FUNK!	160,763,000
7	FETTY WAP FT. REMY BOYZ	679	155,994,000
8	JUSTIN BIEBER	WHAT DO YOU MEAN?	154,446,000
9	SKRILLEX & DIPLO FT. JUSTIN BIEBER	WHERE ARE Ü NOW	153,575,000
10	THE WEEKND	EARNED IT (FIFTY SHADES OF GREY)	151,941,000

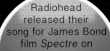

Radiohead released their song for James Bond film *Spectre* on **DEC 25, 2015**

THE WEEKND

6 Canadian artist Ab I Makkonen Tesfaye aka The Weeknd has won 19 international music awards since 2012.

ED SHEERAN

7 "Thinking Out Loud" won two awards, Song of the Year and Best Pop Solo Performance, at the 58th Grammy Awards, held in Los Angeles, California, USA on February 15, 2016.

TOP 10

MOST ON-DEMAND STREAMED VIDEOS 2015

People are streaming on-demand music videos more than ever, with figures that have more than doubled since last year's *Top 10 of Everything* book...

	ARTIST(S)	SONG	TOTAL ON-DEMAND VIDEO STREAMS
1	SILENTÓ	WATCH ME (WHIP/NAE NAE)	487,490,000
2	FETTY WAP	TRAP QUEEN	401,621,000
3	MARK RONSON FT. BRUNO MARS	UPTOWN FUNK!	395,045,000
4	WIZ KHALIFA FT. CHARLIE PUTH	SEE YOU AGAIN	327,156,000
5	TAYLOR SWIFT	SHAKE IT OFF	237,745,000
6	THE WEEKND	THE HILLS	236,514,000
7	ED SHEERAN	THINKING OUT LOUD	204,804,000
8	ADELE	HELLO	198,963,000
9	TAYLOR SWIFT	BLANK SPACE	192,930,000
10	OMARION FT. CHRIS BROWN & JHENE AIKO	POST TO BE	192,681,000

BIGGEST-SELLING DIGITAL SONGS 2015

TOP 10

When you consider that the most downloaded song (The Black Eyed Peas' 2009 hit "I Gotta Feeling") has sold 8.77 million copies, these 2015 hits' sales are huge...

	ARTIST(S)	SONG	TOTAL SALES
1	MARK RONSON FT. BRUNO MARS	UPTOWN FUNK!	5,529,000
2	ED SHEERAN	THINKING OUT LOUD	3,976,000
3	WIZ KHALIFA FT. CHARLIE PUTH	SEE YOU AGAIN	3,801,000
4	ADELE	HELLO	3,712,000
5	MAROON 5	SUGAR	3,343,000
6	WALK THE MOON	SHUT UP AND DANCE	2,986,000
7	FETTY WAP	TRAP QUEEN	2,730,000
8	OMI	CHEERLEADER	2,698,000
9	THE WEEKND	THE HILLS	2,586,000
10	TAYLOR SWIFT FT. KENDRICK LAMAR	BAD BLOOD	2,580,000

OMI

8 Jamaican singer OMI, aka Omar Samuel Pasley, initially independently released "Cheerleader" in 2012. Its 2014 remix by German producer Felix Jaehn led to it being a worldwide hit the following year.

WALK THE MOON

6 This band have been performing since 2008. Electronic duo The Knocks invited Walk The Moon to appear on their song "Best For Last", taken from their 2016 album 55.

In 2015, individual digital tracks by Taylor Swift sold: **10,563,000**

KENDRICK LAMAR

7 The Compton, California, USA-born artist won five of his 11 Grammy Award nominations in 2016, including Best Rap Album for To Pimp A Butterfly.

CHRIS STAPLETON

10 Although *Traveller* is the country and blues artist's debut album, he has written more than 150 songs for other artists over the past 15 years.

ALBUMS OF 2015

This highlight's the success of Adele's *25*...

ADELE, 25
2,307,000

DRAKE, IF YOU'RE READING THIS, IT'S TOO LATE
985,000

TAYLOR SWIFT, 1989
938,000

JUSTIN BIEBER, PURPOSE
768,000

ED SHEERAN, X
546,000

Drake And Future's collaboration was released on **SEP 20, 2015**

TOP 10

BIGGEST-SELLING DIGITAL ALBUMS 2015

Although Drake and Taylor Swift had a hugely successful 2015, the year really did belong to British singer Adele...

	ARTIST(S)	ALBUM	TOTAL SALES
1	ADELE	25	2,307,000
2	DRAKE	IF YOU'RE READING THIS, IT'S TOO LATE	985,000
3	TAYLOR SWIFT	1989	938,000
4	JUSTIN BIEBER	PURPOSE	768,000
5	ED SHEERAN	X	546,000
6	VARIOUS	FIFTY SHADES OF GREY (SOUNDTRACK)	538,000
7	KENDRICK LAMAR	TO PIMP A BUTTERFLY	516,000
8	THE WEEKND	BEAUTY BEHIND THE MADNESS	514,000
9	DRAKE AND FUTURE	WHAT A TIME TO BE ALIVE	508,000
10	CHRIS STAPLETON	TRAVELLER	411,000

On Instagram, Taylor Swift follows **82** accounts

SELENA GOMEZ

2 The Texan singer has crafted more than 1,100 Instagram posts. She follows 227 Instagram accounts. Music aside, Gomez also has 36 movie and television acting credits.

TOP 10

MOST INSTAGRAM FOLLOWERS

Since its launch on October 6, 2010, this platform for sharing photos and videos is more popular than ever...

	ARTIST	HANDLE	FOLLOWERS
1	TAYLOR SWIFT	@TAYLORSWIFT	62,160,814
2	SELENA GOMEZ	@SELENAGOMEZ	59,983,864
3	BEYONCÉ	@BEYONCÉ	56,383,235
4	ARIANA GRANDE	@ARIANAGRANDE	55,300,941
5	JUSTIN BIEBER	@JUSTINBIEBER	53,065,722
6	NICKI MINAJ	@NICKIMINAJ	44,607,258
7	KATY PERRY	@KATYPERRY	37,138,677
8	MILEY CYRUS	@MILEYCYRUS	34,299,597
9	RIHANNA	@BADGALRIRI	31,782,746
10	DEMI LOVATO	@DDLOVATO	31,387,158

DEMI LOVATO

10 Before being a pop star, Lovato's acting career began by playing Angela on children's TV show *Barney & Friends*, which also featured a young Selena Gomez.

Number of studio albums released by Prince:

39

MOST STREAMED MUSIC GENRES

TOP 10

The order has changed since last year, but the top three genres remain the most streamed...

	GENRE	% OF TOTAL STREAMS
1	R&B/HIP-HOP	21.1
▷ 2	ROCK	17.5
3	POP	14.5
4	LATIN	8.5
5	DANCE/ELECTRONIC	4.7
6	COUNTRY	4.1
7	CHRISTIAN/GOSPEL	2.1
8	HOLIDAY/SEASONAL	0.8
▶ 9	CLASSICAL	0.7
10	CHILDREN/JAZZ	0.6

FIGHTSTAR (ROCK)

2 Members of this British rock band are involved with other music projects including Gunship, Once Upon A Dead Man, and Busted, and production company Horsie In The Hedge.

ANDRÉ RIEU (CLASSICAL)

9 The highly acclaimed Dutch violinist and conductor (born October 1, 1949) has been playing the violin since he was five years old. He has also recorded/been involved with more than 50 albums.

JUSTIN TIMBERLAKE

6

Timberlake joined Twitter in March 2009. Since then he has tweeted more than 3,150 times. The singer also has 29 acting credits since his debut in *Model Behavior* (2000).

Total tweets related to the 57th Grammy Awards during broadcast:
13,432,000

POP & GENDER

This illustrates the difference in Twitter followers...

- FEMALE **8**
- MALE **2**

TOP 10

MOST TWITTER FOLLOWERS (SOLO)

By a huge proportion, female pop stars remain the most followed musical artists on Twitter...

	ARTIST	HANDLE	FOLLOWING	FOLLOWERS
1	KATY PERRY	@KATYPERRY	158	80,463,295
2	JUSTIN BIEBER	@JUSTINBIEBER	250,366	73,000,392
3	TAYLOR SWIFT	@TAYLORSWIFT13	245	68,960,677
4	RIHANNA	@RIHANNA	1,152	54,466,304
5	LADY GAGA	@LADYGAGA	131,319	54,145,051
6	JUSTIN TIMBERLAKE	@JTIMBERLAKE	117	51,075,241
7	BRITNEY SPEARS	@BRITNEYSPEARS	396,245	43,719,438
8	SELENA GOMEZ	@SELENAGOMEZ	1,284	37,203,150
9	SHAKIRA	@SHAKIRA	178	36,209,530
10	ARIANA GRANDE	@ARIANAGRANDE	67,918	35,317,805

SHAKIRA

9

Tweeting from her official account since June 2009, the Colombian artist enjoys posting Vines (micro-video loops). Shakira's tweets include 315,000 Vines.

PARAMORE

9 Lead singer Hayley Williams dueted with her life-long friend, fellow musical artist Joy Williams in 2014. A re-recorded version of Paramore's "Hate To See Your Heart Break" was featured on the deluxe edition of the band's self-titled fourth album.

MOST TWITTER FOLLOWERS (BANDS/GROUPS)

TOP 10

Their number of followers (and the amount of accounts they're following) has changed since last year, but the order of artists has not...

	ARTIST(S)	HANDLE	FOLLOWING	FOLLOWERS
1	ONE DIRECTION	@ONEDIRECTION	4,006	26,557,595
2	COLDPLAY	@COLDPLAY	1,482	16,180,666
3	MAROON 5	@MAROON5	405	12,319,760
4	LMFAO	@LMFAO	1,548	8,426,929
5	5 SECONDS OF SUMMER	@5SOS	33,448	8,212,582
6	THE BLACK EYED PEAS	@BEP	47,443	5,307,188
7	LINKIN PARK	@LINKINPARK	49	4,904,829
8	GREEN DAY	@GREENDAY	64	3,999,882
9	PARAMORE	@PARAMORE	173	3,906,781
10	ZOÉ	@ZOETHEBAND	173	3,840,856

Percentage of people in the USA who discover new music via radio: **61%**

COLDPLAY

2 The band, formed in London, England in 1996, have tweeted more than 5,250 times since January 2009. Their seventh studio album, *A Head Full Of Dreams*, was released on December 4, 2015.

213

Total studio albums by the Jackson 5 and Michael Jackson: **28**

MICHAEL JACKSON

4 Known around the world as the King of Pop, Michael Jackson was born on August 29, 1958 and died on June 25, 2009. His short film *Ghosts* (1996) is the longest music video ever made, at almost 40 minutes.

MOST FACEBOOK LIKES (SOLO)

TOP 10

Examining all of the official Facebook Pages for music stars, these are the most Liked...

	SOLO ARTISTS	"LIKES"
1	SHAKIRA	104,236,839
2	EMINEM	92,310,593
3	RIHANNA	81,515,390
4	MICHAEL JACKSON	76,025,671
5	JUSTIN BIEBER	74,648,772
6	BOB MARLEY	74,563,616
7	TAYLOR SWIFT	73,967,026
8	KATY PERRY	71,915,270
9	BEYONCÉ	63,881,972
10	ADELE	63,542,817

KATY PERRY

8 Combining Katy Perry's followers on Twitter, Facebook, Instagram, and YouTube, the American singer's total social media reach exceeds 211 million.

THE BEATLES

3 What began as The Quarrymen (started by John Lennon) in 1956 developed into The Beatles by 1960. Bass guitar player Paul McCartney's 60+-year career has made more than 60 studio albums.

Number of years Linkin Park have been a band:

21

TOP 10

MOST FACEBOOK LIKES (BANDS/ GROUPS)

This chart includes a very broad range of musical genres...

	BAND/GROUP	"LIKES"
1	LINKIN PARK	63,133,705
2	THE BLACK EYED PEAS	45,959,676
▶ 3	THE BEATLES	42,265,928
4	MAROON 5	39,157,063
5	ONE DIRECTION	38,813,650
6	COLDPLAY	38,219,751
7	METALLICA	37,462,288
8	GREEN DAY	32,060,364
9	LMFAO	31,721,688
▷ 10	AC/DC	30,249,581

AC/DC

10 Formed in 1973, the Australian rock band have sold more than 150 million albums worldwide. Their seventeenth album, *Rock or Bust*, was released on November 28, 2014.

MOST SUBSCRIBED MUSIC YOUTUBE CHANNELS

TOP 10

The subscribers of these channels receive alerts when their favourite artists upload new videos...

	ARTIST(S)	SUBSCRIBERS
1	ONE DIRECTION	18,488,817
▶ 2	RIHANNA	18,231,407
3	TAYLOR SWIFT	17,742,236
4	KATY PERRY	17,653,205
5	JUSTIN BIEBER	17,261,956
6	EMINEM	17,201,060
▷ 7	SKRILLEX	11,984,257
8	DAVID GUETTA	10,166,192
9	NICKI MINAJ	10,007,754
10	PENTATONIX	9,923,589

YouTube was founded on
FEB 14, 2005

SKRILLEX

7 Sonny John Moore (aka Skrillex) is most famous for making dubstep. He has collaborated with heavy rock band Korn on their 2011 album *The Path of Totality*, as well as hip-hop artist A$AP Rocky for his 2013 debut *LONG.LIVE.A$AP*.

RIHANNA

2 Born in Barbados on February 20, 1988, Rihanna has released eight studio albums since her 2005 debut, *Music of the Sun*. She has appeared in over 50 music videos. 2016's "Work" single featured Canadian artist Drake.

JUSTIN BIEBER

5 Born March 1, 1994, Canadian Justin Bieber has released four studio albums since his 2010 debut *My World 2.0*. 2015's *Purpose* featured guest performances by Big Sean, Travis Scott, Halsey, and Skrillex.

Apple Music was launched **JUN 30, 2015**

MEGHAN TRAINOR

10 "All About That Bass" was released on June 30, 2014. It was the first single from Meghan Trainor's fourth album *Title* (2015). Its music video was directed by award-winning Fatima Robinson.

PSY'S BIG LEAD

Taylor Swift's "Blank Space" needs 1.2 billion more views...

GANGNAM STYLE 2,493,009,939

BLANK SPACE 1,390,955,285

SEE YOU AGAIN 1,328,732,185

UPTOWN FUNK! 1,275,655,404

BABY 1,274,782,558

TOP 10

OFFICIAL MUSIC VIDEOS WITH THE MOST VIEWS

Although hundreds of music videos were released in 2015, only one was watched enough times to make it into this top 10...

	SONG	ARTIST(S)	DATE UPLOADED	VIEWS
1	GANGNAM STYLE	PSY	JUL 15, 2012	2,493,009,939
2	BLANK SPACE	TAYLOR SWIFT	NOV 10, 2014	1,390,955,285
3	SEE YOU AGAIN	WIZ KHALIFA FT. CHARLIE PUTH	APR 6, 2015	1,328,732,185
4	UPTOWN FUNK!	MARK RONSON FT. BRUNO MARS	NOV 19, 2014	1,275,655,404
5	BABY	JUSTIN BIEBER FT. LUDACRIS	FEB 19, 2010	1,274,782,558
6	SHAKE IT OFF	TAYLOR SWIFT	AUG 18, 2014	1,256,908,141
7	DARK HORSE	KATY PERRY FT. JUICY J	FEB 20, 2014	1,240,231,174
8	BAILANDO	ENRIQUE IGLESIAS FT. DESCEMER BUENO & GENTE DE ZONA	APR 11, 2014	1,236,121,125
9	ROAR	KATY PERRY	SEP 5, 2013	1,213,111,251
10	ALL ABOUT THAT BASS	MEGHAN TRAINOR	JUN 1, 2014	1,202,513,937

In 2015, hip-hop increased in radio airplay popularity by **12%**

ELLIE GOULDING

9 The British singer's debut release was the 2009 EP *An Introduction to Ellie Goulding*. Her third full-length album, *Delirium*, was released on November 6, 2015.

Z KHALIFA

6 "See You Again" (ft. Charlie Puth) was featured on the soundtrack to *Furious 7*. It was written to honour *Fast & Furious* star Paul Walker who died before the seventh movie was completed.

TOP 10

MOST RADIO IMPRESSIONS OF 2015

If you heard any of these hit song played on a radio station, you experienced it clock up another impression towards these huge figures...

	ARTIST(S)	SONG	TOTAL RADIO IMPRESSIONS
1	MARK RONSON FT. BRUNO MARS	UPTOWN FUNK!	4,804,496,000
2	WALK THE MOON	SHUT UP AND DANCE	3,981,730,000
3	ED SHEERAN	THINKING OUT LOUD	3,586,173,000
4	MAROON 5	SUGAR	3,470,501,000
5	TAYLOR SWIFT	STYLE	3,163,189,000
6	WIZ KHALIFA FT. CHARLIE PUTH	SEE YOU AGAIN	3,140,899,000
7	JASON DERULO	WANT TO WANT ME	3,071,643,000
8	THE WEEKND	EARNED IT (FIFTY SHADES OF GREY)	2,928,354,000
9	ELLIE GOULDING	LOVE ME LIKE YOU DO	2,928,018,000
10	THE WEEKND	CAN'T FEEL MY FACE	2,900,066,000

Total tweets related to the 2015 MTV Video Music Awards during broadcast:
21,356,000

BEATS 1 WITH ZANE LOWE

Apple Music's radio station Beats 1 airs continuously in over 100 countries. New Zealander DJ Zane Lowe is one of the station's key curators.

TOP 10

TOP RADIO FORMATS OF 2015 (18-34)

Pop remains, by a great distance, the most listened-to genre on radio...

	FORMAT	% MARKET SHARE (18–34-YEAR-OLDS)
1	POP CONTEMPORARY HIT RADIO	12.4
2	COUNTRY	9.1
3	HOT ADULT CONTEMPORARY	7.6
4	URBAN CONTEMPORARY	6.5
5	ADULT CONTEMPORARY	6.4
6	RHYTHMIC CONTEMPORARY HIT RADIO	5.8
7	ALTERNATIVE	5
8	MEXICAN REGIONAL	4.6
9	CLASSIC ROCK	4.5
10	NEWS TALK	3.6

TAE DYE (COUNTRY)

2 With Madison Marlow, Taylor "Tae" Dye is one half of country duo Maddie & Tae. Their debut album *Start Here* was released August 28, 2015.

GALANTIS (DANCE/ELECTRONIC)

6 This Swedish duo is Linus Eklöw (also know by his moniker Style of Eye) and Christian Karlsson from Miike Snow. Their mascot character is called the Seafox.

SEVENDUST (ROCK)

1 Hailing from Atlanta, Georgia, USA, Sevendust have released 11 studio albums since 1997. Their song "Thank You" (taken from 2015 album *Kill The Flaw*) was nominated Best Metal Performance for the 2016 Grammy Awards.

TOP 10

MOST POPULAR GENRES

The genre with guitar riffs and driving drum sections remains the most popular...

Of total music consumption, children's music represents

1.1%

	GENRE	% OF TOTAL CONSUMPTION
1	ROCK	24.5
2	R&B/HIP-HOP	18.2
3	POP	15.7
4	COUNTRY	8.5
5	LATIN	4.5
6	DANCE/ELECTRONIC	3.4
7	CHRISTIAN/GOSPEL	2.8
8	HOLIDAY/SEASONAL	1.7
9	JAZZ	1.3
=	CLASSICAL	1.3

GENRE BREAKDOWN

Here's how the top five compare visually...

ROCK 24.5

R&B/HIP-HOP 18.2

POP 15.7

COUNTRY 8.5

LATIN 4.5

TOP 10

BIGGEST-SELLING ALBUMS EVER

The accurate sales figures of albums and singles started in 1991 via SoundScan, and these are the 10 most successful sellers...

	ARTIST(S)	ALBUM	YEAR RELEASED	TOTAL SALES
1	METALLICA	METALLICA	1991	16,218,000
2	SHANIA TWAIN	COME ON OVER	1997	15,629,000
3	ALANIS MORISSETTE	JAGGED LITTLE PILL	1995	15,045,000
4	THE BEATLES	BEATLES 1	2000	12,659,000
5	BACKSTREET BOYS	MILLENNIUM	1999	12,262,000
6	WHITNEY HOUSTON/VARIOUS	THE BODYGUARD (SOUNDTRACK)	1992	12,187,000
7	BOB MARLEY & THE WAILERS	LEGEND	1984	11,924,000
8	SANTANA	SUPERNATURAL	1999	11,892,000
9	CREED	HUMAN CLAY	1999	11,710,000
10	ADELE	21	2011	11,453,000

Alanis Morissette has released

32

singles

SHANIA TWAIN

2

On March 3, 2015, Shania Twain released *Still The One: Live From Vegas*. The DVD edition includes 25 tracks and celebrated the 105 shows she performed as part of her residency at Las Vegas's The Colosseum at Caesar's Palace between 2012–14.

THE BEATLES

4

In 2016, former Beatle Paul McCartney created instrumental tunes to accompany animated emojis for communication application Skype.

OUTER
SPACE

ZONE **9**

Dwarf planet Haumea was discovered on **DEC 28, 2004**

CERES

1 On March 6, 2015, NASA's space probe Dawn (launched on September 27, 2007) was caught in Ceres' gravity. It became the first man-made craft to successfully orbit a dwarf planet in our solar system.

TOP 10

SMALLEST PLANETS/DWARF PLANETS IN OUR SOLAR SYSTEM

As there are only eight planets in our solar system, dwarf planets are needed for this Top 10...

	PLANET/ DWARF PLANET	DIAMETER (KM)	(MI)
1	CERES	950	590
2	MAKEMAKE	1,422	883.59
3	HAUMEA	1,960	1,217
4	ERIS	2,326	1,445.3
5	PLUTO	2,368	1,471.4
6	MERCURY	4,878	3,031
7	MARS	6,792	4,220
8	VENUS	12,104	7,521
9	EARTH	12,720	7,904
10	NEPTUNE	49,528	30,775

TOP 5 SMALLEST

Here is how their diameters compare graphically...

CERES 590 MI
MAKEMAKE 883.59 MI
HAUMEA 1,217 MI
ERIS 1,445.3 MI
PLUTO 1,471.4 MI

MAKEMAKE

2 In Earth years, it take dwarf planet Makemake 310 years to orbit the Sun. Makemake resides in the Kuiper Belt, an area of space just outside Neptune's orbit.

VENUS

2 Although Mars is the planet we talk about the most, Venus is actually Earth's closest neighbour. After the Sun and the Moon, it is also the brightest thing in the sky.

TOP 10

FASTEST PLANETS/ DWARF PLANETS ORBITING OUR SUN

If you consider we call the time it takes Earth to orbit the Sun a "year", check out how long these "years" are...

	PLANET/DWARF PLANET	DAYS TO ORBIT THE SUN
1	MERCURY	87.97
2	VENUS	224.7
3	EARTH	365.26
4	MARS	686.98
5	CERES	1,680.19
6	JUPITER	4,332.82
7	SATURN	10,755.7
8	URANUS	30,687.15
9	NEPTUNE	60,190.03
10	PLUTO	90,553.02

Scientists estimate the Sun formed over **4.6 BILLION** years ago

MERCURY

1 On March 6, 2013, NASA's robot spacecraft MESSENGER successfully completed a first full mapping of the planet. Mercury's surface looks a lot like our Moon's.

TOP 10

PLANETS/DWARF PLANETS FURTHEST FROM OUR SUN

Dwarf planets Makemake and Eris were only discovered 11 years ago in 2005...

NAME	TYPE	DISTANCE FROM THE SUN (KM)	(MI)
1 ERIS	DWARF PLANET	10,210,000,000	6,344,199,872.7
2 MAKEMAKE	DWARF PLANET	6,850,000,000	4,256,392,666.8
3 HAUMEA	DWARF PLANET	6,484,000,000	4,028,970,810.5
▶ **4** PLUTO	DWARF PLANET	5,906,380,000	3,670,054,382.4
5 NEPTUNE	PLANET	4,498,252,900	2,795,084,767.5
6 URANUS	PLANET	2,870,972,200	1,783,939,418.8
7 SATURN	PLANET	1,426,725,400	886,526,062.8
8 JUPITER	PLANET	778,412,010	483,682,798.7
9 CERES	DWARF PLANET	413,700,000	257,061,262.2
▷ **10** MARS	PLANET	227,936,640	141,633,261.8

PLUTO

4 This, the most famous of the dwarf planets, has five moons: Charon (the largest), Hydra, Kerberos, Nix, and Styx.

You share living on Earth with approx.

7.3
BILLION
other humans

MARS

10 The red planet's Mariner Valley is 2,500 miles (4,023 km) long. Including projects across all space agencies, there have been 44 missions to learn about Mars.

233

TOP 10

PLANETS/DWARF PLANETS WITH LONGEST DAYS

Counting from sunrise to night to the following sunrise, look at how long days are in the top three...

	PLANET/DWARF PLANET	HOURS PER DAY
1	MERCURY	4,222.6
2	VENUS	2,802
3	PLUTO	153.28
4	ERIS	25.9
5	MARS	24.66
▸ 6	EARTH	23.93
7	URANUS	17.24
8	NEPTUNE	16.11
▸ 9	SATURN	10.66
10	JUPITER	9.93

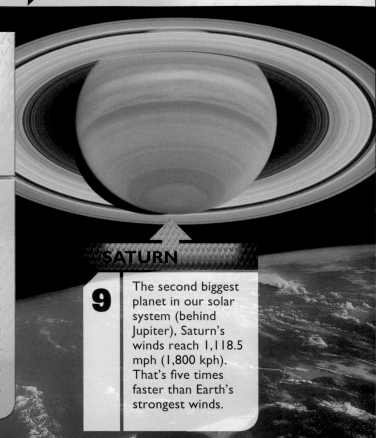

SATURN

9 The second biggest planet in our solar system (behind Jupiter), Saturn's winds reach 1,118.5 mph (1,800 kph). That's five times faster than Earth's strongest winds.

EARTH

6 On October 24, 1946, a V-2 rocket captured the first photo of our planet from space. On November 5, 2013, an Earth-sized planet, Kepler-78b, was found outside our solar system.

DAYS COMPARED

As a bar chart, here is how the top 5 look...

MERCURY
4,222.6

VENUS
2,802

PLUTO
153.28

ERIS
25.9

MARS
24.66

From midnight to midnight on Mercury, you would experience

175.9
Earth days

PLANETS/DWARF PLANETS WITH THE BIGGEST SURFACE AREA

You could stretch 125 copies of Earth's surface around the vastness of Jupiter...

	NAME	TYPE	SURFACE AREA (KM²)	(MI²)
1	JUPITER	PLANET	64,000,000,000	24,710,538,146.7
2	SATURN	PLANET	44,000,000,000	16,988,494,975.8
3	URANUS	PLANET	8,100,000,000	3,127,427,484.2
4	NEPTUNE	PLANET	7,700,000,000	2,972,986,620.8
5	EARTH	PLANET	510,000,000	196,912,100.9
6	VENUS	PLANET	460,000,000	177,606,992.9
7	MARS	PLANET	140,000,000	54,054,302.2
8	MERCURY	PLANET	75,000,000	28,957,661.9
9	PLUTO	DWARF PLANET	17,700,000	6,834,008.2
10	ERIS	DWARF PLANET	17,000,000	6,563,736.7

URANUS

3 On January 24, 1986, NASA space probe Voyager 2 captured close-up views of Uranus, including its clouds. Methane gives the planet its blue appearance.

JUPITER

1 The largest planet in our solar system is famous for its large red spot. Not a surface marking, this is actually a huge swirling storm twice the width of Earth.

Dwarf planet Eris was first discovered **JAN 5, 2005**

235

MAKEMAKE

Missing out on this Top 10, dwarf planet Makemake has a surface temperature of -398.2°F (-239°C). Pronounced "mah-kee-mah-kee", it is named after the Rapanui's (natives of Easter Island) god of fertility.

VENUS

1

The highest point on Venus is Maxwell Montes, which is 6.8 miles (11 km) high. To date, there have been 41 missions to study more about Venus.

TOP 10

PLANETS/DWARF PLANETS WITH HOTTEST SURFACE TEMPERATURE

Humans would have to develop special technology to survive these brutal temperatures...

	NAME	TYPE	SURFACE TEMPERATURE (°C)	(°F)
1	VENUS	PLANET	462	863.6
2	MERCURY	PLANET	(-173 TO) 427	(-279.4 TO) 800.6
3	EARTH	PLANET	(-88 TO) 58	(-126.4 TO) 136.4
4	MARS	PLANET	(-87 TO) -5	(-124.6 TO) 23
5	CERES	DWARF PLANET	-105	-157
6	JUPITER	PLANET	-108	-162.4
7	SATURN	PLANET	-139	-218.2
8	URANUS	PLANET	-197	-322.6
9	NEPTUNE	PLANET	-201	-329.8
10	PLUTO	DWARF PLANET	-229	-380.2

Venus' diameter is only **403.89** MI less than Earth's

MARS

7 The image of Mars' surface was taken by NASA's Mars Pathfinder. The craft deployed a robotic rover called Sojourner which explored the planet for 83 days in 1997.

Mars has **2** moons

TOP 10

PLANETS/DWARF PLANETS WITH STRONGEST GRAVITY

You would have great difficulty jumping high on Jupiter, and could float away on Pluto...

	NAME	TYPE	EQUATORIAL GRAVITY (M/S^2)
1	**JUPITER**	PLANET	**23.12**
2	**NEPTUNE**	PLANET	**11**
3	**SATURN**	PLANET	**10.44**
4	**EARTH**	PLANET	**9.81**
5	**VENUS**	PLANET	**8.87**
6	**URANUS**	PLANET	**8.69**
7	**MARS**	PLANET	**3.71**
8	**MERCURY**	PLANET	**3.70**
9	**HAUMEA**	DWARF PLANET	**0.63**
10	**PLUTO**	DWARF PLANET	**0.62**

NEPTUNE

2 In 1989, NASA's Voyager 2 captured this image of Neptune's largest moon, Triton. Neptune has 13 confirmed moons, with a 14th waiting to be officially classified.

GRAVITY EXPLAINED

Gravity is a naturally occurring phenomenon. It causes the tidal cycles of the oceans, and is what gives objects their different weights. The stronger the gravity is on a planet, the "heavier" objects would feel.

LONGEST RUNNING
OPERATIONAL SPACE AGENCIES

The space race continues to be expensive and competitive, with these nations the longest participants...

	AGENCY	COUNTRY	YEAR FOUNDED
1	INTA (INSTITUTO NACIONAL DE TÉCNICA AEROESPACIAL)	SPAIN	1942
2	NASA (NATIONAL AERONAUTICS & SPACE ADMINISTRATION)	USA	1958
3	CNES (NATIONAL CENTRE OF SPACE RESEARCH)	FRANCE	1961
=	SUPARCO (SPACE AND UPPER ATMOSPHERE RESEARCH COMMISSION)	PAKISTAN	1961
5	DLR (GERMAN AEROSPACE CENTER)	GERMANY	1969
=	ISRO (INDIAN SPACE RESEARCH ORGANISATION)	INDIA	1969
7	SNSB (SWEDISH NATIONAL SPACE BOARD)	SWEDEN	1972
8	ESA (EUROPEAN SPACE AGENCY)	(EUROPEAN SYNDICATION)	1975
9	ASI (ITALIAN SPACE AGENCY)	ITALY	1988
10	CSA (CANADIAN SPACE AGENCY)	CANADA	1989

Valentina Tereshkova was the first woman sent into space: **JUN 16, 1963**

KARI (KOREA AEROSPACE RESEARCH INSTITUTE)

Founded October 10, 1989, KARI missed out on a place in the above Top 10 chart by just seven months. The agency plans to launch its second rocket, KSLV-2, by 2020.

NASA

2 The 9th Administrator of NASA, Daniel S. Goldin, holds the record for the longest term. He performed the role for 3,517 days between April 1, 1992 and November 17, 2001.

247

MICE

9 This photo shows American Colonel John P. Stapp and engineer Charles Wade inspecting the "Mousenick" space capsule before its space mission.

2 bullfrogs were sent into space on

NOV 9, 1970

TOP 10

FIRST LIVING THINGS IN SPACE

The original heroes for providing scientists key intel about space? This array of organisms...

	ORGANISM	ROCKET	DATE
1	FRUIT FLIES	V2	FEB 20, 1947
2	MOSS	V2	VARIOUS, 1947
3	RHESUS MONKEY (ALBERT II)	V2	JUNE 14, 1949
4	MOUSE	V2	AUG 31, 1950
5	DOG (LAIKA)	SPUTNIK 2	NOV 3, 1957
6	SQUIRREL MONKEY (GORDO)	JUPITER IRBM AM-13	DEC 13, 1958
7	RABBIT (MARFUSA)	R2	JULY 2, 1959
8	CHIMPANZEE (HAM)	REDSTONE	JAN 31, 1961
9	GUINEA PIGS, FROGS & MICE	VOSTOK 3A	MARCH 1961
10	TORTOISE	ZOND 5	SEP 18, 1968

DOG

5 Laika was a stray dog that made history by being the first dog in space. She died within hours, but this wasn't revealed to the public until 2002. She has a monument in Moscow in her honour.

MOST TIME SPENT IN SPACE (MULTIPLE MISSIONS)

All of these astronauts have spent at least 18 months in space, and some nearly 2.5 years...

	NAME	COUNTRY	FLIGHTS	TOTAL TIME IN SPACE (DAYS)
1	GENNADY PADALKA	RUSSIA	5	879.5
2	SERGEI KRIKALEV	RUSSIA*	6	803.4
3	ALEXANDR KALERI	RUSSIA	5	769.3
4	SERGEI AVDEYEV	RUSSIA*	3	747.6
5	VALERI POLYAKOV	RUSSIA*	2	678.7
6	ANATOLY SOLOVYEV	RUSSIA*	5	651.1
7	YURI MALENCHENKO	RUSSIA	5	641.5
8	VIKTOR AFANASYEV	RUSSIA*	4	555.8
9	YURY USACHEV	RUSSIA	4	552.8
10	PAVEL VINOGRADOV	RUSSIA	3	546.9

* Includes mission(s) during Soviet Union era.

GENNADY PADALKA

1 During his time in space, Padalka worked on both the ISS and the Mir space station. He also clocked up 10 EVA (Extra-vehicular Activity) tasks.

ANATOLY SOLOVYEV

6 The above photo captures the moment just before Anatoly Solovyev and Pavel Vinogradov boarded the Soyuz TM-26 spacecraft on August 5, 1997.

PAVEL VINOGRADOV

10 The Russian Soyuz TM-26 spacecraft that took Vinogradov and Solovyev to Mir was the 32nd mission to the space station. The mission was completed on February 19, 1998.

With Ekaterina Dmitrieva in Texas, Yuri Malenchenko married her via satellite from on board the ISS on

AUG 10, 2003

249

CHARLES DUKE

10 Born October 3, 1935, Charles Duke holds the record for being the youngest astronaut to walk on the moon. He was 36 years old.

BUZZ ALDRIN

2 The second man to walk on the moon has published two autobiographies, *Return To Earth* (1973) and *Magnificent Desolation: The Long Journey Home from the Moon* (2009).

Retired astronaut Edgar Mitchell's total time in space:

9 DAYS
1 MINUTE

TOP 10

FIRST HUMANS TO WALK ON THE MOON

Our moon is the only celestial body that humankind has made physical contact with, for now...

	NAME	COUNTRY	MISSION	DATE WALKED ON THE MOON
1	NEIL ARMSTRONG	USA	APOLLO 11	JULY 21, 1969
▶ 2	BUZZ ALDRIN	USA	APOLLO 11	JULY 21, 1969
3	PETE CONRAD	USA	APOLLO 12	NOV 19–20, 1969
4	ALAN BEAN	USA	APOLLO 12	NOV 19–20, 1969
5	ALAN SHEPARD	USA	APOLLO 14	FEB 5–6, 1971
6	EDGAR MITCHELL	USA	APOLLO 14	FEB 5–6, 1971
7	DAVID SCOTT	USA	APOLLO 15	JULY 31–AUG 2, 1971
8	JAMES IRWIN	USA	APOLLO 15	JULY 31–AUG 2, 1971
9	JOHN W. YOUNG	USA	APOLLO 16	APR 21–23, 1972
▶ 10	CHARLES DUKE	USA	APOLLO 16	APR 21–23, 1972

NASA

1

The first iteration of the US space agency was NACA (National Advisory Committee for Aeronautics), founded March 3, 1915.

TOP 10

BIGGEST SPACE PROGRAMS

Adventures into the black vastness of space are a high priority for these nations' agencies...

	AGENCY	COUNTRY	BUDGET ($ MILLIONS)
1	**NASA** (NATIONAL AERONAUTICS & SPACE ADMINISTRATION)	USA	**18,500**
2	**ROSCOSMOS** (RUSSIAN FEDERAL SPACE AGENCY)	RUSSIA	**5,600**
3	**ESA** (EUROPEAN SPACE AGENCY)	(EUROPEAN SYNDICATION)	**5,510**
4	**CNES** (NATIONAL CENTRE OF SPACE RESEARCH)	FRANCE	**2,500**
5	**JAXA** (JAPAN AEROSPACE EXPLORATION AGENCY)	JAPAN	**2,460**
6	**DLR** (GERMAN AEROSPACE CENTER)	GERMANY	**2,000**
7	**ASI** (ITALIAN SPACE AGENCY)	ITALY	**1,800**
8	**CNSA** (CHINA NATIONAL SPACE ADMINISTRATION)	CHINA	**1,780**
9	**ISRO** (INDIAN SPACE RESEARCH ORGANISATION)	INDIA	**1,200**
10	**CSA** (CANADIAN SPACE AGENCY)	CANADA	**488.7**

ROSCOSMOS

2

Founded on February 25, 1992, this Russian space agency took over from the Soviet Space Program which was operational for 60 years, between 1931 and 1991.

AGENCIES SIDE BY SIDE

Here's how the biggest 5 compare...

NASA
$18,500 MILLION

ROSCOSMOS
$5,600 MILLION

ESA
$5,510 MILLION

CNES
$2,500 MILLION

JAXA
$2,460 MILLION

Total ESA member states:

22

Total Space Invaders games across all platforms:
46

ASTEROIDS

7 The highest score ever achieved playing Asteroids is 41,338,740 by John McAllister on April 6, 2010. The previous world record had not been beaten for over 27 years.

ASTEROIDS

ATARI

• Explosive rapid-fire space action • 1 or 2 players are challenged to destroy asteroids and enemy spacecraft • New Atari-designed QuadraScan™ display system • New personal high score table display • Optional "Hyperspace" • Optional coinage including Susan B. Anthony coin slot • Bonus play at 10,000 points.

TOP 10

OLDEST ARCADE GAMES SET IN SPACE

The multi-billion-dollar video game industry has its roots in simple, but highly effective arcade classics...

	NAME	DEVELOPED BY	RELEASE DATE
1	GALAXY GAME	BILL PITTS & HUGH TUCK	SEP 1971
2	COMPUTER SPACE	NOLAN BUSHNELL & TED DABNEY	NOV 1971
3	ASTRO RACE	TAITO	JUL 1973
4	SPACE WARS	CINEMATRONICS	OCT 1977
5	SPACE INVADERS	TAITO	JUL 1978
6	GALAXIAN	NAMCO	OCT 1979
7	ASTEROIDS	ATARI	NOV 1979
=	TAIL GUNNER	VECTORBEAM	NOV 1979
9	DEFENDER	WILLIAMS ELECTRONICS	FEB 1981
10	ELIMINATOR	SEGA	DEC 1981

SPACE-WARS

Sonic

SPACE WAR

SPACE WARS

4 Unlike other arcade games of the 1970s, Space Wars could not be played as a solo game. It was designed for two people to battle each other.

STAR WARS BATTLEFRONT

3 More than two years in the making, this, the third in the series (but considered a reset) was released on November 17, 2015 for PS4, Xbox One, and PC platforms.

TOP 10

MOST GROSSING STAR WARS VIDEO GAMES

The Force awakened in 2015, but it has been strong with video gamers for decades...

	NAME	GENRE	PLATFORM	RELEASED	UNIT SALES ($MILLIONS)
1	LEGO STAR WARS: THE COMPLETE SAGA	ACTION	WII	2007	5.57
2	LEGO STAR WARS: THE COMPLETE SAGA	ACTION	DS	2007	4.73
3	STAR WARS BATTLEFRONT	SHOOTER	PS2	2004	3.61
4	STAR WARS BATTLEFRONT II	SHOOTER	PS2	2005	3.59
5	LEGO STAR WARS: THE VIDEO GAME	ACTION	PS2	2005	3.53
6	STAR WARS: EPISODE III – REVENGE OF THE SITH	ACTION	PS2	2005	3.32
7	STAR WARS: EPISODE I RACER	RACING	N64	1999	3.12
8	STAR WARS: THE FORCE UNLEASHED	ACTION	XBOX 360	2008	2.71
9	LEGO STAR WARS II: THE ORIGINAL TRILOGY	ACTION	PS2	2006	2.69
10	STAR WARS: SHADOWS OF THE EMPIRE	ACTION	N64	1996	2.65

Across all gaming platforms,

230

Star Wars games have been made

LEGO STAR WARS: THE COMPLETE SAGA

1 Released across eight platforms between 2007 and 2015, this 2012 Kids' Choice Award-winning game features LEGO spins on the Star Wars films, Episodes I to VI.

MOVIES & TV

ZONE 10

TOP 10

BIGGEST MOVIES OF ALL TIME

Comparing every film ever made from around the world, these are the most successful...

	MOVIE	YEAR OF RELEASE	BOX OFFICE ($ WORLDWIDE)
1	AVATAR	2009	2,787,965,087
2	TITANIC	1997	2,186,772,302
▶ 3	STAR WARS: EPISODE VII – THE FORCE AWAKENS	2015	2,028,057,964
▷ 4	JURASSIC WORLD	2015	1,670,400,637
5	THE AVENGERS	2012	1,519,557,910
6	FURIOUS 7	2015	1,514,827,481
7	AVENGERS: AGE OF ULTRON	2015	1,405,413,868
8	HARRY POTTER AND THE DEATHLY HALLOWS: PART 2	2011	1,341,511,219
9	FROZEN	2013	1,276,480,335
10	IRON MAN 3	2013	1,215,439,994

James Spader (who played Ultron in the Avengers sequel) has **55** acting credits

JURASSIC WORLD

4 This, the fourth *Jurassic Park* film, holds the record for the biggest opening weekend for a summer movie. The website JurassicWorld.com is created as an in-world experience, as though the park is real.

STAR WARS: EPISODE VII – THE FORCE AWAKENS

3 *Episode VII* broke dozens of box office records around the world. In the US, it's the most successful movie of all time. It also holds the US record for the biggest opening day, weekend, and first week.

STEVEN SPIELBERG

1 This American filmmaker directed many of the most iconic and influential films of all time, including *Jaws* (1975), the *Indiana Jones* movies, and *Jurassic Park* (1993). Spielberg also asked J.J. Abrams if he would direct *Star Wars: Episode VII – The Force Awakens*.

Francis Lawrence (director of the last three *Hunger Games* films) total box office:
$3,204,946,658

DIRECTORS BY COUNTRY

Here's how the below list looks by nation...

- ■ USA **6**
- ■ UK **2**
- ■ CANADA **1**
- ■ NZ **1**

J.J. ABRAMS

The eleventh most successful film director of all time is J.J. Abrams. His five films total $3,539,065,992 at the worldwide box office. He also has a further 44 producer credits and 21 writing credits.

TOP 10

MOST SUCCESSFUL DIRECTORS OF ALL TIME

Behind every hit blockbuster is a team of thousands of people, all led by the film's director...

	NAME	COUNTRY	TOTAL FILMS DIRECTED (THEATRICALLY RELEASED)	BOX OFFICE ($ WORLDWIDE)
1	STEVEN SPIELBERG	USA	29	9,508,961,476
2	PETER JACKSON	NEW ZEALAND	14	6,530,713,297
3	JAMES CAMERON	CANADA	10	6,207,806,867
4	MICHAEL BAY	USA	12	5,775,726,013
5	CHRISTOPHER NOLAN	UK	9	4,227,531,716
6	DAVID YATES	UK	6	4,176,096,940
7	ROBERT ZEMECKIS	USA	17	4,139,921,474
8	CHRIS COLUMBUS	USA	15	4,099,031,132
9	GEORGE LUCAS	USA	6	3,997,678,795
10	TIM BURTON	USA	18	3,803,729,658

DANCES WITH WOLVES

5 Kevin Costner starred in and directed this winner of seven Oscars. Michael Blake wrote the screenplay based on his own novel.

Peter *"Lord of the Rings"* Jackson's debut feature film, *Bad Taste* (an alien invasion horror comedy), was made in

1987

BIGGEST BEST PICTURE OSCAR WINNERS

Of all the movies that were awarded Best Picture, these ones made the most at the box office...

SLUMDOG MILLIONAIRE

7 Dev Patel and Freida Pinto both made their feature film acting debuts in this film. It won eight Academy Awards and was based on Vikas Sawrup's 2005 novel *Q & A.*

	MOVIE	YEAR WON ACADEMY AWARD FOR BEST PICTURE	BOX OFFICE ($ WORLDWIDE)
1	TITANIC	1997	2,186,772,302
2	THE LORD OF THE RINGS: THE RETURN OF THE KING	2003	1,119,929,521
3	FORREST GUMP	1994	677,945,399
4	GLADIATOR	2000	457,640,427
5	DANCES WITH WOLVES	1990	424,208,848
6	THE KING'S SPEECH	2010	414,211,549
7	SLUMDOG MILLIONAIRE	2008	377,910,544
8	AMERICAN BEAUTY	1999	356,296,601
9	RAIN MAN	1988	354,825,435
10	SCHINDLER'S LIST	1993	321,306,305

MOST MARVEL/DC CHARACTER MOVIE APPEARANCES

Find out where your favourite movie/comic book character ranks below...

	CHARACTER	NO. OF MOVIE APPEARANCES
1	BATMAN	10
2	WOLVERINE	8
=	CHARLES XAVIER	8
=	SUPERMAN	8
5	CAPTAIN AMERICA	7
=	IRON MAN	7
=	SPIDER-MAN	7
=	MAGNETO	7
9	JEAN GREY	6
=	MYSTIQUE	6

WOLVERINE

2 Australian actor Hugh Jackman dons the claws for a final time in the 2017 *Wolverine* film, directed by James Mangold.

Along with her Jean Grey/ *X-Men* films, Famke Janssen has

57

acting credits

OFF-THE-CHART ENTRIES

Let's not forget these three key characters...

BLACK WIDOW
5

STORM
5

PEGGY CARTER
4

MYSTIQUE

9 *The Hunger Games* saga's Jennifer Lawrence has portrayed the younger iteration of Raven Darkholme/Mystique three times. Rebecca Romijn has played her four times.

269

NICK FURY

Samuel L. Jackson has appeared as Nick Fury in eight Marvel productions (seven movies and the TV series *Agents of S.H.I.E.L.D.*). The Washington, D.C.-born actor has acted in more than 160 different productions.

TOP 10

BIGGEST MARVEL MOVIES

Of all the comic-book adaptions, characters and stories from Marvel publications rule the box office...

	MOVIE	YEAR OF RELEASE	BOX OFFICE ($ WORLDWIDE)
1	THE AVENGERS	2012	1,519,557,910
2	AVENGERS: AGE OF ULTRON	2015	1,405,035,767
3	IRON MAN 3	2013	1,215,439,994
4	SPIDER-MAN 3	2007	890,871,626
5	SPIDER-MAN	2002	821,708,551
6	SPIDER-MAN 2	2004	783,766,341
7	GUARDIANS OF THE GALAXY	2014	773,312,399
8	THE AMAZING SPIDER-MAN	2012	757,930,663
9	X-MEN: DAYS OF FUTURE PAST	2014	747,862,775
10	CAPTAIN AMERICA: THE WINTER SOLDIER	2014	714,421,503

X-Men Apocalypse was released **MAY 1, 2016**

THE AVENGERS

1 The fifth most successful film of all time, *The Avengers* is one of only 24 movies to make more than $1 billion at the box office worldwide. It was director Joss Whedon's second feature film of the four he's made.

THE DARK KNIGHT

2 Australian actor Heath Ledger posthumously won the 2009 Oscar for Best Supporting Actor for his portrayal of The Joker in the second film of the *Dark Knight* trilogy.

Batman (1989) was composer Danny Elfman's

11TH

feature film score of his 100 credits

MAN OF STEEL

3 Including voice artists, 11 different actors have played Superman. Henry Cavill made his Clark Kent debut in *Man of Steel*, and continued the role in *Batman v Superman: Dawn of Justice* (2016).

TOP 10

BIGGEST DC MOVIES

Prior to 2016's *Batman v Superman: Dawn of Justice*, these are the most lucrative DC movies...

	MOVIE	YEAR OF RELEASE	BOX OFFICE ($ WORLDWIDE)
1	THE DARK KNIGHT RISES	2012	1,084,939,099
2	THE DARK KNIGHT	2008	1,004,558,444
3	MAN OF STEEL	2013	668,045,518
4	BATMAN	1989	411,348,924
5	SUPERMAN RETURNS	2006	391,081,192
6	BATMAN BEGINS	2005	374,218,673
7	BATMAN FOREVER	1995	336,529,144
8	SUPERMAN	1978	300,218,018
9	BATMAN RETURNS	1992	266,822,354
10	BATMAN AND ROBIN	1997	238,207,122

BIGGEST INDEPENDENT CREATOR-OWNED MOVIES

A "creator-owned" comic features stories wholly produced/owned by an independent creator...

	MOVIE	PUBLISHER(S)	YEAR OF RELEASE	BOX OFFICE ($ WORLDWIDE)
1	TEENAGE MUTANT NINJA TURTLES	MIRAGE STUDIOS/IDW	2014	493,333,584
2	THE MASK	DARK HORSE	1994	351,583,407
3	WANTED	TOP COW	2008	341,433,252
4	THE GREEN HORNET	DYNAMITE	2011	227,817,248
5	TEENAGE MUTANT NINJA TURTLES	MIRAGE STUDIOS/IDW	1990	201,965,915
6	HELLBOY II: THE GOLDEN ARMY	DARK HORSE	2008	160,388,063
7	JUDGE DREDD	FLEETWAY/REBELLION	1995	113,493,481
8	HELLBOY	DARK HORSE	2004	99,318,987
9	TMNT	MIRAGE STUDIOS/IDW	2007	95,608,995
10	SPAWN	IMAGE	1997	87,840,042

Dredd (2012) starred Karl Urban and Lena Headey and made

$35,626,525

THE MASK

2 The comic was first published in 1987. Jim Carrey portrayed the character for the 1994 film, which also marked the acting debut of Cameron Diaz.

30 DAYS OF NIGHT

Just off the chart is director David Slade's adaptation of the vampiric comic *30 Days Of Night* (2002) by Steve Niles and Ben Templesmith. Released 2007, it made $75,505,973 at the box office.

WATCHMEN

5 Zack Snyder (*Batman v Superman: Dawn of Justice*) directed this movie adaptation of the graphic novel by Alan Moore and Dave Gibbons.

PUBLISHING COMPARISON

More DC-connected creator-owned titles have been successful films...

■ DC **7**
■ MARVEL **3**

BIGGEST CREATOR-OWNED MOVIES
(BASED ON MARVEL OR DC COMIC/IMPRINT)

These creator-owned comics (turned movies) had Marvel/DC publishing support...

	MOVIE	PUBLISHER(S)	YEAR OF RELEASE	BOX OFFICE ($ WORLDWIDE)
1	MIB 3	AIRCEL/MALIBU/MARVEL	2012	624,026,776
2	MEN IN BLACK	AIRCEL/MALIBU/MARVEL	1997	589,390,539
3	MEN IN BLACK II	AIRCEL/MALIBU/MARVEL	2002	441,818,803
4	RED	HOMAGE/WILDSTORM/DC	2010	199,006,387
5	WATCHMEN	DC	2009	185,258,983
6	ROAD TO PERDITION	PARADOX PRESS/DC	2002	181,001,478
7	THE LEAGUE OF EXTRAORDINARY GENTLEMEN	ABC/WILDSTORM/DC	2003	179,265,204
8	RED 2	HOMAGE/WILDSTORM/DC	2013	148,075,565
9	STARDUST	VERTIGO/DC	2007	135,560,026
10	V FOR VENDETTA	VERTIGO/DC	2006	132,511,035

V FOR VENDETTA

10 The comic was published in different forms between 1982–89. The film's screenplay was written by the Wachowskis, the siblings behind *The Matrix* franchise.

The first issue of *Red* (by Warren Ellis and artist Cully Hamner) was published in

2003

INSIDE OUT

10 This, the fifteenth Disney Pixar movie, won 47 international film awards. It was released five months before their sixteenth film, *The Good Dinosaur*.

Minions + Despicable Me 1 & 2 total box office: **$2,672,970,113**

ICE AGE: CONTINENTAL DRIFT

9 The fourth *Ice Age* movie was the most successful animated film of 2012. Its sequel, *Ice Age: Collision Course* was released on June 30, 2016.

TOP 10

BIGGEST ANIMATED MOVIES

Examining all of the different kinds of animated film ever made, these are the 10 box-office smashes...

	MOVIE	YEAR OF RELEASE	BOX OFFICE ($ WORLDWIDE)
1	FROZEN	2013	1,276,480,335
2	MINIONS	2015	1,159,094,243
3	TOY STORY 3	2010	1,063,171,911
4	THE LION KING	1994	987,483,777
5	DESPICABLE ME 2	2013	970,761,885
6	FINDING NEMO	2003	936,743,261
7	SHREK 2	2004	919,838,758
8	ICE AGE: DAWN OF THE DINOSAURS	2009	886,686,817
9	ICE AGE: CONTINENTAL DRIFT	2012	877,244,782
10	INSIDE OUT	2015	856,809,711

BIGGEST CELL/TRADITIONAL ANIMATED MOVIES

Making animated tales with hand-drawn/painted still images pre-dates CGI (computer-generated imagery)...

	MOVIE	YEAR OF RELEASE	BOX OFFICE ($ WORLDWIDE)
1	THE LION KING	1994	987,483,777
2	THE SIMPSONS MOVIE	2007	527,071,022
3	ALADDIN	1992	504,050,219
4	TARZAN	1999	448,191,819
5	BEAUTY AND THE BEAST	1991	424,967,620
6	POCAHONTAS	1995	346,079,773
▶ 7	WHO FRAMED ROGER RABBIT?	1988	329,803,958
8	THE HUNCHBACK OF NOTRE DAME	1996	325,338,851
9	MULAN	1998	304,320,254
▷ 10	SPIRITED AWAY	2002	274,925,095

WHO FRAMED ROGER RABBIT?

7 Filmmaker Robert Zemeckis followed up *Back to the Future* (1985) with this fusion of live-action and cell animation. Both movies starred Christopher Lloyd.

SPIRITED AWAY

10 Studio Ghibli's twelfth feature is its most successful film. It won the 2003 Academy Award for Best Animated Feature, and a further 53 international film awards.

The Emperor's New Groove (2000) total box office: **$169,327,687**

LONGEST-RUNNING US ANIMATED TV SERIES

These popular animated shows also count among some of the most successful TV shows of all time...

	TV SHOW	YEARS ON AIR	TOTAL EPISODES
1	THE SIMPSONS	1989–PRESENT	595+
2	FAMILY GUY	1999–2003; 2005–PRESENT	274+
3	SOUTH PARK	1997–PRESENT	267+
4	KING OF THE HILL	1997–2010	259
5	ARTHUR	1996–PRESENT	227+
6	BEAVIS AND BUTT-HEAD	1993–97; 2011	222
7	ADVENTURE TIME	2007; 2010–PRESENT	219+
8	AMERICAN DAD!	2005–PRESENT	210+
9	SPONGEBOB SQUAREPANTS	1999–PRESENT	200+
10	TEENAGE MUTANT NINJA TURTLES	1987–96	193

SOUTH PARK

3 Matt Stone and Trey Parker's TV show also spawned the animated feature film *South Park: Bigger, Longer & Uncut.* It made $83,137,603 at the box office worldwide.

THE SIMPSONS

1 This franchise's spin-off video games have sold more than 21 million units. Universal Studios Hollywood features a recreation of the town of Springfield.

Number of *Adventure Time* seasons to date:

7

4 MORE HITS

Here's how 4 other popular cartoons compare to the top 10...

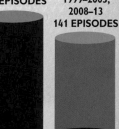

FUTURAMA 1999–2003; 2008–13 **141 EPISODES**

DORA THE EXPLORER 1999; 2000–13 **172 EPISODES**

RUGRATS 1991–2003 **172 EPISODES**

THE FLINTSTONES 1999–2003; 2008–13 **141 EPISODES**

DORAEMON

2 Aside from the hit TV show, the time-travelling robotic cat Doraemon has also starred in 37 feature films and over 80 video games.

SAZAE-SAN

6 Created, written, and illustrated by Japanese artist Machiko Hasegawa in 1946, the animated TV series of her manga comic began in October 1969.

A live-action feature film of *Nintama Rantarō* was released in

2011

TOP 10

LONGEST-RUNNING ANIME TV SERIES

Japanese animation is a popular art form and industry the world over, as these stats prove...

	TV SHOW	YEARS ON AIR	TOTAL EPISODES
1	SAZAE-SAN	1969–PRESENT	7,332+
2	DORAEMON	1973; 1978; 1979–2005; 2005–PRESENT	2,561+
3	NINTAMA RANTARŌ	1993–PRESENT	1,878+
4	OYAKO CLUB	1994–2013	1,818
5	KIRIN NO MONOSHIRI YAKATA	1975–79	1,565
6	OJARUMARU	1998–PRESENT	1,551+
7	KIRIN ASHITA NO CALENDAR	1980–84	1,498
8	MANGA NIPPON MUKASHI BANASHI	1975–85	1,488
9	HOKA HOKA KAZOKU	1976–82	1,428
10	SOREIKE! ANPANMAN	1988–PRESENT	1,315+

CORPSE BRIDE

5 Oscar-nominated actor Helena Bonham-Carter provided the voice for the Corpse Bride in this stop-motion feature. Her love interest, Victor Van Dort, was voiced by fellow Oscar-nominee Johnny Depp.

Wallace & Gromit's first adventure was *A Grand Day Out*, which debuted on

DEC 24, 1990

TOP 10

BIGGEST STOP-MOTION ANIMATED MOVIES

This style of animation incorporates numerous still photos, edited to create movement...

	MOVIE	YEAR OF RELEASE	BOX OFFICE ($ WORLDWIDE)
1	CHICKEN RUN	2000	224,834,564
2	WALLACE & GROMIT: THE CURSE OF THE WERE-RABBIT	2005	192,610,372
3	CORALINE	2009	124,596,398
4	THE PIRATES! IN AN ADVENTURE WITH SCIENTISTS!	2012	123,054,041
5	CORPSE BRIDE	2005	117,195,061
6	THE BOXTROLLS	2014	109,285,033
7	PARANORMAN	2012	107,139,399
8	SHAUN THE SHEEP MOVIE	2015	83,475,982
9	FRANKENWEENIE	2012	81,491,068
10	THE NIGHTMARE BEFORE CHRISTMAS	1993	75,082,668

THE BOXTROLLS

6 This is based on British novelist Alan Snow's book *Here Be Monsters!* (2005). It was produced by Laika, the studio behind *ParaNorman* (2012) and *Coraline* (2009).

TOP 10

BIGGEST ANIME MOVIES

Japan's Studio Ghibli is responsible for six of the films in this top 10...

	MOVIE	YEAR OF RELEASE	BOX OFFICE ($ WORLDWIDE)
1	SPIRITED AWAY	2002	274,925,095
2	HOWL'S MOVING CASTLE	2005	235,184,110
3	PONYO	2009	201,750,937
4	POKÉMON: THE FIRST MOVIE	1999	163,644,662
5	PRINCESS MONONOKE	1999	159,375,308
6	THE SECRET WORLD OF ARRIETTY	2012	145,570,827
7	POKÉMON: THE MOVIE 2000	2000	133,949,270
8	THE WIND RISES	2013	117,932,401
9	STAND BY ME, DORAEMON	2014	105,100,000
10	ONE PIECE FILM: Z	2012	72,822,122

THE WIND RISES

8 The nineteenth Studio Ghibli animated feature film debuted in Japan on July 20, 2013. The USA release included the vocal talents of Emily Blunt.

Dragon Ball Z: Resurrection 'F' released in 2015 made
$61,768,190
at the box office

PONYO

3 This was written and directed by Studio Ghibli co-founder Hayao Miyazaki. It won 11 international film awards, including Animation of the Year at the 2009 Tokyo Anime Awards.

FIRST EVER MOVIES BASED ON VIDEO GAMES

Long before the 2016 adaptation of *Assassin's Creed*, came these video game movies...

	MOVIE	BASED ON GAME FRANCHISE	RELEASED
1	SUPER MARIO BROS.: THE GREAT MISSION TO RESCUE PRINCESS PEACH!	SUPER MARIO BROS.	JUL 20, 1986
=	RUNNING BOY STAR SOLDIER	STAR SOLDIER	JUL 20, 1986
3	SUPER MARIO BROS.	SUPER MARIO BROS.	MAY 28, 1993
4	FATAL FURY: THE MOTION PICTURE	FATAL FURY	JUL 16, 1994
5	STREET FIGHTER II: THE ANIMATED MOVIE	STREET FIGHTER II	AUG 8, 1994
6	DOUBLE DRAGON	DOUBLE DRAGON	NOV 4, 1994
7	STREET FIGHTER	STREET FIGHTER	DEC 23, 1994
8	MORTAL KOMBAT	MORTAL KOMBAT	AUG 18, 1995
9	MORTAL KOMBAT: ANNIHILATION	MORTAL KOMBAT	NOV 21, 1997
10	POKÉMON: THE FIRST MOVIE	POKÉMON	JUL 18, 1998

MORTAL KOMBAT: ANNIHILATION

9 The first *Mortal Kombat* video game was released in 1992. After the initial movie adaptation made $122,195,920 at the box office, the 1997 sequel achieved $51,376,861.

STREET FIGHTER

7 1994's *Street Fighter* starred Jean-Claude Van Damme as Guile. It took $99,423,521 at the box office worldwide. 2009's *Street Fighter: The Legend of Chun-Li* made $12,764,201.

Number of *Pokémon* movies made:

18

Number of *Digimon* movies made:

9

GAMES ON TV

This bar chart reflects the popularity of each gaming franchise...

POKÉMON
940+
EPISODES

DIGIMON
332
EPISODES

KIRBY:
RIGHT
BACK AT
YA!
100
EPISODES

SATURDAY
SUPERCADE
97
EPISODES

SONIC X
78
EPISODES

MEGA MAN STAR FORCE

6 One of Capcom's most famous characters was designed by Akira Kitamura and Keiji Inafune. Mega Man is the star of more than 100 games across all major platforms.

KIRBY: RIGHT BACK AT YA!

3 Created by Japanese game designer Masahiro Sakurai, the Kirby franchise has sold 36.2 million copies of games worldwide.

TOP 10

LONGEST-RUNNING TV SHOWS BASED ON VIDEO GAMES

The *Pokémon* brand is a force to be reckoned with in the TV industry as well as the gaming world...

	TV SHOW	BASED ON GAME FRANCHISE	YEARS ON AIR	TOTAL EPISODES
1	POKÉMON	POKÉMON	18 (1997–PRESENT)	940+
2	DIGIMON	DIGIMON	12 (1999–2011)	332
3	KIRBY: RIGHT BACK AT YA!	KIRBY	2 (2001–3)	100
4	SATURDAY SUPERCADE	VARIOUS	2 (1983–85)	97
5	SONIC X	SONIC THE HEDGEHOG	2 (2003–5)	78
6	MEGA MAN STAR FORCE	MEGA MAN	2 (2006–8)	76
7	MONSTER RANCHER	MONSTER RANCHER	2 (1999–2001)	73
8	ADVENTURES OF SONIC THE HEDGEHOG	SONIC THE HEDGEHOG	3 (1993–96)	67
9	THE SUPER MARIO BROS. SUPER SHOW!	SUPER MARIO BROS.	1 (1989)	65
10	BOMBERMAN JETTERS	BOMBERMAN	1 (2002–3)	52

WRECK-IT RALPH

1 The cast of this Disney movie features comedic actors from acclaimed movies and TV shows, including: John C. Reilly (*Step Brothers*), Sarah Silverman (*Bob's Burgers*), Jack McBrayer (*30 Rock*), and Jane Lynch (*Role Models*).

The Angry Birds Movie was released on

MAY 11, 2016

SPY KIDS 3D: GAME OVER

4 Filmmaker Robert Rodriguez, the man behind *Sin City* (2005) and its sequel, wrote and directed four *Spy Kids* movies between 2001 and 2011. They grossed a box-office total of $550,233,830.

TOP 10

BIGGEST MOVIES ABOUT VIDEO GAMING

These original tales were all inspired from the technology and tales from the video game industry...

	MOVIE	YEAR OF RELEASE	BOX OFFICE ($ WORLDWIDE)
1	WRECK-IT RALPH	2012	471,222,889
2	TRON LEGACY	2010	400,062,763
3	PIXELS	2015	244,150,128
4	SPY KIDS 3D: GAME OVER	2003	197,011,982
5	WARGAMES	1983	79,567,667
6	SCOTT PILGRIM VS. THE WORLD	2010	47,664,559
7	TRON	1982	33,000,000
8	THE LAST STARFIGHTER	1984	28,733,290
9	STAY ALIVE	2006	27,105,095
10	AVALON	2001	15,740,796

BIGGEST VIDEO GAME MOVIE ADAPTATIONS

Dozens of hit gaming series have been made into big-screen adventures, and these are the box-office hits...

	MOVIE	YEAR OF RELEASE	BASED ON GAME FRANCHISE	BOX OFFICE ($ WORLDWIDE)
1	PRINCE OF PERSIA: THE SANDS OF TIME	2010	PRINCE OF PERSIA	336,365,676
2	RESIDENT EVIL: AFTERLIFE	2010	RESIDENT EVIL	296,221,663
3	LARA CROFT: TOMB RAIDER	2001	TOMB RAIDER	274,703,340
4	RESIDENT EVIL: RETRIBUTION	2012	RESIDENT EVIL	240,159,255
5	NEED FOR SPEED	2014	NEED FOR SPEED	203,277,636
6	POKÉMON: THE FIRST MOVIE	1998	POKÉMON	163,644,662
7	LARA CROFT TOMB RAIDER: THE CRADLE OF LIFE	2003	TOMB RAIDER	156,505,388
8	RESIDENT EVIL: EXTINCTION	2007	RESIDENT EVIL	147,717,833
9	POKÉMON: THE MOVIE 2000	1999	POKÉMON	133,949,270
10	RESIDENT EVIL: APOCALYPSE	2004	RESIDENT EVIL	129,394,835

Hitman: Agent 47 (2015) total box office: **$82,347,656**

PRINCE OF PERSIA: THE SANDS OF TIME

1 Inspired by the 2003 video game of the same name, Jake Gyllenhaal plays Prince Dastan. His first film role was as the son of Billy Crystal's character in *City Slickers* (1991).

RESIDENT EVIL: RETRIBUTION

4 This is the fifth movie in the series. The sixth, *Resident Evil: The Final Chapter* is set for a 2017 release.

Into the Woods received **60** international award nominations

GREASE

3 John Farrar's "Hopelessly Devoted To You" was nominated for Best Original Song at the 1979 Academy Awards. In the 2016 TV movie *Grease: Live*, Canadian singer-songwriter Carly Rae Jepsen played Frenchy.

TOP 10

MOST SUCCESSFUL MUSICALS

The 10 biggest musical movies cover everything from colleges, puppets, and magic....

	MOVIE	YEAR OF RELEASE	BOX OFFICE ($ WORLDWIDE)
1	MAMMA MIA!	2008	609,841,637
2	LES MISÉRABLES	2012	441,809,770
3	GREASE	1978	394,955,690
4	ENCHANTED	2007	340,487,652
5	CHICAGO	2002	306,776,732
6	HIGH SCHOOL MUSICAL 3: SENIOR YEAR	2008	252,909,177
7	INTO THE WOODS	2014	213,116,401
8	HAIRSPRAY	2007	202,548,575
9	MOULIN ROUGE	2001	179,213,434
10	THE MUPPETS	2011	165,184,237

ENCHANTED

4 Amy Adams, who plays lead character Giselle, has been nominated for an Academy Award five times. Her 53 acting credits include Lois Lane in *Batman v Superman: Dawn of Justice* (2016).

JURASSIC WORLD

1 The mock-real *Jurassic World* website describes its genetic creation the Indominus Rex as 40 ft (12.2 m) long. It states its roar reaches 160 decibels, which matches a 747 plane taking off.

Classic eighties dinosaur movie *Baby: Secret of the Lost Legend* (1985) total box office: **$14,972,297**

TOP 10
BIGGEST PREHISTORIC MOVIES
All four of the *Jurassic Park* franchise movies feature here, totalling $3,686,974,327...

	MOVIE	YEAR OF RELEASE	BOX OFFICE ($ WORLDWIDE)
1	JURASSIC WORLD	2015	1,670,400,637
2	JURASSIC PARK	1993	1,029,153,882
3	ICE AGE: DAWN OF THE DINOSAURS	2009	886,686,817
4	THE LOST WORLD: JURASSIC PARK	1997	618,638,999
5	JURASSIC PARK III	2001	368,780,809
6	DINOSAUR	2000	349,822,765
7	THE GOOD DINOSAUR	2015	294,191,192
8	THE LAND BEFORE TIME	1988	84,460,846
9	LAND OF THE LOST	2009	68,777,554
10	WALKING WITH DINOSAURS	2013	61,021,593

THE GOOD DINOSAUR

7 The Disney Pixar film won three Animated Feature awards at the 2016 VES (Visual Effects Society) for Visual Effects, Effects Simulations, and Created Environment.

BIG ASS SPIDER!

Stars Greg Grunberg (*Star Wars: Episode VII – The Force Awakens*) and Lombardo Boyar (*Murder in the First*) both feature in the 2015 anthology film *Tales of Halloween*.

The original Universal Studios *The Wolf Man* was released

DEC 9, 1941

DEEP BLUE SEA

8

Beyond the sharks in this film, actor Thomas Jane has faced a gigantic bear in *Into the Grizzly Maze* (2015) and dimensional creatures in *The Mist* (2007).

TOP 10

MOST SUCCESSFUL CREATURE FEATURES (NON-DINO AND NON ALIEN/ PREDATOR FRANCHISES)

Not counting dino movies or the *Alien* and *Predator* franchises, these creature movies are the 10 biggest...

	MOVIE	YEAR OF RELEASE	BOX OFFICE ($ WORLDWIDE)
1	KING KONG	2005	550,517,357
2	GODZILLA	2014	529,076,069
3	JAWS	1977	470,653,000
4	PACIFIC RIM	2013	411,002,906
5	GODZILLA	1998	379,014,294
6	SUPER 8	2011	260,095,986
7	CLOVERFIELD	2008	170,764,026
▶ 8	DEEP BLUE SEA	1999	164,648,142
9	GREMLINS	1985	153,083,102
10	THE WOLFMAN	2010	139,789,765

OFF-THE-CHART ENTRIES

Here are the next 10 most successful monster movies...

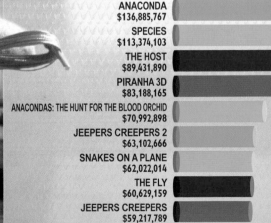

ANACONDA
$136,885,767

SPECIES
$113,374,103

THE HOST
$89,431,890

PIRANHA 3D
$83,188,165

ANACONDAS: THE HUNT FOR THE BLOOD ORCHID
$70,992,898

JEEPERS CREEPERS 2
$63,102,666

SNAKES ON A PLANE
$62,022,014

THE FLY
$60,629,159

JEEPERS CREEPERS
$59,217,789

THE MIST
$57,293,715

INDEX BY A–Z

PICTURE CREDITS

T: top **B:** bottom **L:** left **C:** center **R:** right **BG:** background

ACKNOWLEDGMENTS

Paul Terry would like to thank: all of the contributing sources, especially paleobiologists Luke Hauser and David Martill, Anna Loynes and Nielsen for the music intel, and the brilliant IMDb and VGChartz teams; my Editor extraordinaire Polly Poulter for knocking another T-10 book out of the park; my brilliant Editorial Director Trevor Davies for the ongoing support (and film recommendations); Team T-10's designer, picture researchers, sub-editors, proofreaders, and marketeers for all their hard work; all at Octopus Books and Readerlink; and as always, a massive thank you to my frequent collaborator Tara Bennett for all the support and encouragement while I juggled these facts and stats alongside our other creature-filled projects.

DATA SOURCES:

Pages: 11, 16, 17, 24, 25, 32, 33 – data sourced from Luke Hauser and David Martill, paleobiologists. Pages: 98, 100–127, 253 – data sourced from VGChartz.com Pages: 152–154, 156, 158–163 – data sourced from the Council on Tall Buildings and Urban Habitat. Pages: 204–209, 211, 218–227 – data sourced from Copyright © 2016 The Nielsen Company. All rights reserved. Nielsen and the Nielsen logo are trademarks or registered trademarks of CZT/ACN Trademarks, L.L.C. Other product and service names are trademarks or registered trademarks of their respective companies.15/9032. Pages: 230–237 – data sourced from NASA (https://solarsystem.nasa.gov). Pages: 256–260, 262–265, 268, 270–275, 278–279, 282–299 – data sourced from IMDB.com. Box office information courtesy of The Internet Movie Database (http://www.imdb.com). Used with permission.
The Top 10 team collects data on a rolling basis. All data in this book is the most recent data available at time of going to press.